MAKE TODAY YOUR MASTERPIECE

BOB FASHANO

Editing • Authoring • Traditional and Electronic Publishing

Orchard Park, NY 14127
MediaHatchery.com

ISBN 978-1-955180-08-5

DESIGN BY BILL ZULEWSKI
PHOTOGRAPHY BY KC KRATT + DYLAN BUYSKES

Printed in the United States of America

First Printing, 2022

Media Hatchery
P. O. Box 554
Orchard Park, NY 14127

mediahatchery.com

Table of Contents

CHAPTER TWO

Cultivating Connection

CHAPTER THREE

Mastering Communication

CHAPTER FOUR
Enhancing Coaching

Just Passing Through or Adding Value?

A number of years ago I read a quotation from plantsman and agriculture pioneer George Washington Carver that had a profound impact on me. He said, "No individual has any right to come into the world and go out of it without leaving behind him distinct and legitimate reasons for having passed through it."

For me, this prompts the question: Are we just passing through or are we being intentional and on purpose?

This book is about how important it is to be intentional about today. Every day gives us an opportunity to add value and make a difference in someone's life. Yet, we must not take these opportunities for granted. Daily, we must be intentional about serving and impacting others.

In *The Rubaiyat of Omar Khayyam*, translator Edward Fitzgerald writes,

> *The Moving Finger writes; and, having writ,*
> *Moves on: nor all thy Piety nor Wit*
> *Shall lure it back to cancel half a Line*
> *Nor all thy Tears wash out a Word of it.*

Yesterday is gone forever, perhaps with some limited value of lessons learned. Tomorrow is no guarantee. But today is yesterday's tomorrow and it's all you've got. *What will you do with it?*

We make decisions every day about how we invest our time—With whom? Where? Doing what? How? And why?

When it comes down to it, no matter what our work is, we are all in the people business. We could be mostly solitary farmers, cross-country truck drivers. We could be car dealers or, as in my previous work before I "rewired," provide insurance and financial services—a connection and communication business if ever there was one! But whether we are pulmonologists or personal trainers, teach preschool or make art, stay at home with the kids or travel for work three-quarters of the year, each of us has only today, and, no matter what, every single one of us will affect those around us. Which is why intentionality is key.

Our intentions are the first inklings of our whys. And when we state our intentions and follow through with action, we make manifest our whys and those whys then ripple out and, depending on what we have intended, can make a positive difference in the lives of others—whether family, friends, coworkers or strangers.

What is your *why?*

Author Simon Sinek wrote a bestseller entitled *Start with Why.* In business, this why is called the "mission statement." The religious and spiritual world calls it "your calling." Whichever term you choose, I ask you this: Do you have one? Do you have something that is clear and meaningful to you?

A number of years ago, I came across a template that includes two components to developing the "what's your reason for being" statement:

To (your contribution), so that (your impact).

Getting personal, here's mine:

To *intentionally connect and add value to select individuals,* so that *my influence will help them grow and become all they can be.*

As you can see it is a simple format. I urge you to try it, and then be intentional about living it out.

This book is geared toward helping people to recognize, develop and act out their intentions. It is for leaders. "Leader" generally calls up an image in many people's minds—one's boss or the CEO of a multinational, a politician, perhaps, or the director of a religious or charitable organization or nonprofit. But I tend to interpret "leader" differently: We all have the opportunity to lead. That is, we all have the opportunity to influence others. Those myriad others may populate our "masterpiece" and, as those who've known me for years know, I am fond of saying, "Make Today Your Masterpiece," which always involves making a positive impact on a person, even if this person happens to be you making an impact on yourself.

But there is a lot here for those who are developing themselves as leaders in business, where they may have an executive team and certainly people they may mentor—whether in the workplace or outside.

People want to follow a passionate leader. When leaders are passionate about a topic, it can be contagious. But people also need to follow a leader who also has conviction as well. What's the difference between passion and conviction?

We can be passionate about something and not necessarily have lived it or successfully experienced what it is we are passionate about. It's primarily intellectual. Take sports. A coach who has never played the sport can have a love for it and be passionate about playing hard, preparing and winning, but not felt the highs and lows of being a player. The team feels the difference.

But a coach who has played the game, prepared, practiced and can relate to how his or her players feel, will have a deeper understanding of what the players are experiencing. This coach has conviction, and the players feel it.

Conviction breeds credibility. It is stronger than intellect, stronger than a belief. A conviction can be so strong that it governs your decision in such a way that you are willing to put almost anything on the line for it.

Passion without the experience is just that—passion. When you add passion to conviction, you can inspire. And when you inspire, you can change behavior, and when you change behavior, you can change lives.

This work is for people who want to change lives—starting with their own. The first section details some of the traits and practices helpful for leaders to have and develop so that they can lead better and with more wisdom. From there, I explore three key aspects that are woven through human relationships and are especially important to hone for leaders to succeed with their teams and teams to succeed with their clients and customers: Connection, Communication and Coaching.

In my more than 40 years in business, starting from an advisor position all the way to launching my own agency and developing my successors, understanding how to connect, how to communicate and how to coach—and practicing these every day, *intentionally*—was part of what helped to create our success. It is my fervent hope that by utilizing what I have learned and practicing it themselves, readers might gain a solid foundation in "the three C's" and perhaps shorten the time needed to mature into fine leaders, regardless of their line of work.

Readers will have the opportunity to practice each step, as each one includes a call to action, and following each section, there is space and time for self-reflection and for assessing where they are and where they still need more refining. I like to think of this whole process the way one might think of painting a landscape: The canvas has to be prepared first. From there, strokes build upon strokes. Then, maybe, the light is not quite right, so something needs to be built up and something taken away, and on it goes.

But ask any artist out there whether they are ever satisfied and you may not be surprised to hear, there was always something else they could have done. This is true for all of us working on our masterpieces. Our masterpieces are never finished, but the point is to try to make the best we possibly can with the time and other constraints we have.

"Times are tough." We hear this now more and more, of course. Health. Vast structures, including central governments and global supply lines. We live in a time of unprecedented change. Rather than go with the currents, it is time to be more intentional about our work, to envision that which we really want—from what kind of world we want to live in to the way in which we want to conduct our business and ourselves.

I hope that by using this book and following through on the action steps, you will become more nimble, both as a human being and as a leader.

My mentor John Maxwell, author, pastor and authority on leadership, summed it up best when he said, "When I die, I cannot take with me what I have, but I can live in others by what I gave."

The pages that follow are filled with lessons and insights that, when applied, will help you become fulfilled, optimistic and grateful. So, turn the page and make today your masterpiece.

CHAPTER ONE

Laying the Groundwork

After more than 40 years of leading teams in my own business, leading colleagues in my profession, and leading fellow members of my church, I came to realize that any person has the capacity to lead. It is not that leading comes easily; there is much in our fast-paced culture that leaves little time, space, or energy for everything that goes into leading. But, with a good attitude and consistent practice of the right steps, leading can come more naturally.

My first brush with leadership came in sixth grade. For some crazy reason, my class elected me president. This was not based on my ability to lead. As any young person knows, class leaders typically are chosen based on how popular they are. I knew that. The thing was, being elected class president back then showed me two things: One was, leadership is not based on position or title. A whole lot more goes into the ability to lead than just being given the title of "leader." On the other hand, I saw how being likable was a necessary color in the leadership palette. Likable leaders have greater appeal and an easier time leading.

When I use the word "groundwork," I am saying there are certain aspects of preparation that rightly precede leadership, but depending on one's circumstances—if one is flung into leadership, for example—there may be little time for preparation. But no matter. Make the time, because preparing —laying the groundwork—provides long-term benefits, both personal and professional. What helps us to lay the groundwork includes, among other things, our "why": our recognition of our values, our vision, our mindset, understanding the essential nature of trust, and making time for gratitude.

In this section, you'll have the opportunity to get intentional about leading yourself. You are always the first person you lead, and the more capable and skilled you become at that, the easier and more successful you will be at leading others.

Think of this section as you might a blank canvas. Few artists begin by laying paint on a canvas. There may be hundreds of sketches first. The exercises here are like those sketches and like gessoing the background and starting to rough in what you want the masterpiece to look like —the end included in the beginning, though as humans, we are never finished canvases. After each entry, exercises will help you to apply what you are learning, with whom, and why. The important thing, regardless of when you do them, is to do them.

If you take the exercises seriously and are faithful about completing them and revisiting them, you'll find you have better outcomes as you start to work with others through connecting, communicating, and coaching, which are the focus of the sections that follow.

So, clear your workspace, eliminate distractions, and let's get started.

What Motivates You?

Motivation is a passion for work that goes beyond money and status.

Daniel Goleman, Ph.D., author, *Emotional Intelligence*

That feel-good sweet spot—whatever it is that gets the juices flowing and puts the fire in the belly—is critical to healthy leadership, as well as an important component of emotional intelligence (EI).

You get up every day and want to tackle problems, win new business deals, help another person grow and develop, and serve your clients/customers—that's your motivation. It is that simple. We are best positioned for success when we're passionate and motivated by what we are doing.

So here are the questions: What motivates you? Where will you go for inspiration and momentum? How can you better tap what's already inside of you to revitalize your spirit?

The formula is to link your actions and behavior to your biggest motivating factors to achieve your goals.

Having this level of EI can inform us where it's best to invest our time and where we may want to delegate to allow others to shine.

Here is a quick pulse check:

- Am I energized by helping others grow and develop?
- Do I take an interest in partnering with others to help them solve their problems?
- Do I have a positive outlook, regardless of the circumstances or present challenges?
- Am I driven to find the energy every day to compete and be the best I can be?

Your answers may guide you to a better understanding of your motivation. What are you passionate about? What would you like to improve? Remember, motivation is within your control.

TODAY, I WILL DEVELOP A LIST OF AT LEAST FIVE ASPECTS OF MY WORK THAT GET MY JUICES FLOWING AND BRING ME THE MOST SATISFACTION. OF THESE FIVE, I WILL CHOOSE THREE WITHIN MY CONTROL WHERE I CAN IMPROVE.

I WILL DO THIS THIS WAY:

_____

_____

_____

_____

_____

_____

_____

_____

_____

_____

_____

_____

AND I WILL DO THIS BECAUSE:

_____

_____

_____

_____

_____

How Is Your Intentionality?

Outside my faith, the decision to grow has impacted my life more than any other.

John C. Maxwell, leadership expert and author

As leaders, we have no choice but to grow and develop for the sake of others. To grow and develop, we must be intentional—we must be on a lifelong mission of growth and development.

Yet, there are so often gaps in our intentionality, ways of thinking that stall our growth. Author, speaker, and pastor John C. Maxwell talks about the Law of Intentionality in *The 15 Invaluable Laws of Growth*. He points out that growth doesn't just happen. Many of us have misconceptions about growth that may be holding us back from being as intentional as we should be. These beliefs, he says, create "gaps" that can keep us from growing.

They are:

THE ASSUMPTION GAP	"I assume that I will automatically grow."
THE KNOWLEDGE GAP	"I don't know how to grow."
THE MISTAKE GAP	"I'm afraid of making mistakes."
THE PERFECTION GAP	"I have to find the best way before I start."
THE INSPIRATION GAP	"I don't feel like doing it."
THE COMPARISON GAP	"Others are better than I am."
THE EXPECTATION GAP	"I thought it would be easier than this."

Working on ourselves should be one of our highest priorities. As we humbly acknowledge our gifts are from God, we have a responsibility to further develop them.

When we grow and develop our leadership skills and knowledge, we are best positioned to influence others. They become the recipient, and they, in turn, grow. That is the purpose of leadership: grow and develop more leaders.

*T*ODAY, I WILL TAKE A DEEP DIVE ON MY INTENTIONALITY "GAPS." WHERE DO
I SEE THESE MISCONCEPTIONS AT WORK IN MY OWN LIFE—BOTH IN THE PAST
AND NOW?

I CHOOSE TO WORK ON THIS ONE:

_____

_____

_____

I WILL DO THIS BY:

_____

_____

_____

_____

_____

_____

_____

AND I WILL DO THIS BECAUSE:

_____

_____

_____

_____

Gauge Your Conviction

In a moment of decision, the best thing you can do is the right thing. The worst thing you can do is nothing.

Theodore Roosevelt, 26th U.S. President

As leaders, we need to form the habit of conviction. This is essential for us to be a change agent. If ignored or not developed, conviction can be compromised quickly because every person of influence will face a moment or moments when they will be tempted to compromise their integrity. How many stories have we read or heard about leaders in government, business, or among clergy where their lives—and those they love—were destroyed as a result of their compromise?

A mentor of mine had a mantra that became sticky to me: "There is no right way to do a wrong thing." Please let that sink in. The habit of conviction means always doing what is right—not what is easy. Oh, by the way, a warning: The higher you climb on your leadership journey, the harder it gets.

The first step in developing the habit of conviction is to identify your convictions and values. What do you stand for? What hills will you die on? What is not for sale or non-negotiable? We need to remember—our reputation is not for sale. It takes years to build, but only a few seconds to lose. It is our responsibility to protect it. Bottom line—our best friend is our convictions. When they are lost, the enemy appears, and bad things happen.

All our decisions should be based on what has meaning for us, what is critical, what is non-negotiable. It's been said that when values are clear, decisions are easier. So, we need to identify our personal values, and those must be in alignment with the organization's and our team's values. We are, after all, the organization.

When living our convictions and values, we have three innate tools—a path, a guard and a gauge. Our values guide us. Every journey has a path and living our values keeps us on the right path. Our values also serve to guard us. Living our values helps protect us from compromising core principles, helps us to maintain an unwavering commitment to truth as we know it. And our values offer us a gauge—a measuring stick. And knowing our values helps us to evaluate where we are.

From time to time, it is helpful to check in with our convictions and values. Start today. Ask yourself, "What are my values?" These may include trustworthiness, courage, humility, encouragement, consistency, and compassion. List your top 10.

Next, consider the areas for improvement. Then, determine when to act.

*T*ODAY, I WILL COMMIT TO SHARING MY TOP 10 VALUES WITH:

_____

BECAUSE I NEED IMPROVEMENT, I CHOOSE TO IMPROVE THIS VALUE:

_____

HERE'S HOW I'LL DO THIS:

_____

_____

_____

_____

_____

_____

_____

_____

_____

AND THIS IS WHY I'LL DO THIS:

_____

_____

_____

_____

_____

How Is Your Self-Awareness?

When you can truly understand how others experience your behavior, without defending or judging, you then have the ability to produce a breakthrough in your leadership and team. Everything starts with your self-awareness. You cannot take charge without taking accountability, and you cannot take accountability without understanding how you avoid it.

Loretta Malandro, author and organizational communication expert

The Institute for Health and Human Potential defines emotional intelligence as the ability to recognize, understand and manage our own emotions, and recognize, understand and influence the emotions of others.

That's a lot to digest. In simple terms: we need to be aware of the emotions that drive our behavior and that affect people—positively and negatively—and learn how to manage those emotions, especially under pressure.

The first step toward becoming an emotionally intelligent leader is understanding the components:

- Self-awareness
- Self-management
- Motivation
- Empathy
- Social skills

For many people, including me at the top of the list, we tend to be more comfortable pointing out ways others can change and improve their actions and behaviors. It's harder to think, plan and act in ways that will transform our own reinvention. As leaders, we need to be reminded to look inward at what we need to improve in ourselves. Remember: *The first person you lead is you.*

A good starting place might be to conduct a simple SWOT analysis—strengths, weaknesses, opportunities and threats. List the things you do well, the things you don't do well, the areas in your life where there are opportunities for improvement, and the biggest threats to your happiness, wellness, and success.

Don't be too hard on yourself or dwell too much on weaknesses; you can improve these or perhaps delegate to others. By knowing what you do well and identifying opportunities for growth and improvement, you are on your way to becoming more self-aware.

Next, consider the areas for improvement. Then, determine when to act.

TODAY, I WILL DO MY SWOT ANALYSIS. I WILL DO THIS BY:

_____

_____

_____

_____

_____

_____

_____

_____

_____

CHOOSING SOMEONE WHO IS ALSO SELF-AWARE AND IMPARTIAL,
I WILL KEEP AN OPEN MIND AND RUN MY ANALYSIS BY:

_____

AND THIS IS WHY I'LL DO THIS:

_____

_____

_____

_____

How Is Your Self-Management?

Emotions alert us to specific trouble, and they do so without any subterfuge.
If we're aware enough to listen to them—if our attention is focused and our minds
are centered—our emotions will be able to contribute exactly what we need
to move into and then out of any trouble imaginable.

Karla McLaren, author and educator

Self-management, like motivation and self-awareness, is another key attribute of emotional intelligence. Emotionally intelligent leaders maintain a keen understanding of their strengths and limitations as well as the ability to positively influence the organization and its people.

Self-management has many components. For leaders, adaptability is *not* optional. Every day, we are faced with adversity; and the ability to face challenges head on with confidence and courage is critical. We must maintain a calm, cool, and collected outlook.

Our emotions play a large part in our self-management; allowing emotions to flow means consciously expressing them and gleaning information from them so you can direct that information toward the best outcomes. Blocking or suppressing emotions results in a build-up of stagnant energy that can result in overall stuck behaviors or, if unleashed, the kinds of behaviors that may cause leaders to lose the trust of colleagues, team members, family and friends.

From time to time, it's a good idea to rate yourself on a scale of 1 to 10 (10 being the highest) on your emotions. Of these, which do you allow to flow most and least?

Joy, anger, gratitude, annoyance, grief, serenity, frustration, curiosity, disappointment, hope, hatred, anxiety, sadness, pride, amusement, envy, inspiration, fear, and love.

Of these, choose five that you want to work with in the context of work relationships or relations with family or friends.

$\mathcal{T}$ODAY, I WILL MAKE SOME TIME TO BE QUIET AND CENTER MYSELF, THEN I WILL CHOOSE AN EMOTION TO WORK WITH.

_____

HOW HAVE I BEEN EXPRESSING OR SUPPRESSING THIS EMOTION?

_____

_____

_____

AND IN BOTH CASES, WHAT HAS BEEN THE OUTCOME?

_____

_____

_____

I CAN MANAGE THIS EMOTION BETTER IN THE FOLLOWING WAY(S):

_____

_____

_____

_____

_____

I WILL DO THIS BECAUSE:

_____

_____

_____

Investing or Spending?

I have observed most people put too much emphasis on decision making.
And as a result, they lack focus, discipline, intentionality, and purpose.

John C. Maxwell, leadership expert and author

Time management is another factor in managing ourselves. When I am working with leaders, one of the first things I want to learn is how they manage their time. Is there a plan for prioritizing? We are pulled in so many directions that we need to be aware of the "tyranny of the urgent."

Ask yourself, "Am I spending time or investing time?" When you invest, you expect a rate of return. Which invites you to answer the questions, "what," "with whom," "when," and "how." Caution on spending your time—you may not get a good return. The higher up the so-called ladder you go, the more your responsibilities increase, the harder it becomes to prioritize, yet the more important it becomes so that you get the maximum use of your time for whatever benefit you seek.

*T*ODAY, I WILL CHOOSE ONE SPECIFIC THING TO MAXIMIZE THE RETURN
ON THE TIME I INVEST:

_____

_____

_____

_____

I WILL MAXIMIZE THE RETURN ON THE TIME I INVEST BY:

_____

_____

_____

_____

_____

_____

_____

_____

_____

I WILL DO THIS BECAUSE:

_____

_____

_____

_____

What Business Are You In?

Quality in a service or product is not what you put into it.
It is what the customer gets out of it.

Peter Drucker, management consultant, educator, and author

When you're forming your business plan for the year to come, that's a good time to take stock and ask yourself, "What business am I in?"

The answer has nothing to do with making a profit, though, obviously, you will be out of business if you don't. Profit results from answering the question correctly. Over the years, I have wrestled with this question, but I have discovered a simple answer. For me, "I am in the business of creating customers and satisfying human needs."

As you review your plan, I suggest you filter it through the following:

What is my business?

It is not about your product/service or its name. It is defined by the need the customer satisfies when he/she buys the product/service. The mission and purpose of every business should be to satisfy the customer. We need always to look at the business from the point of view of the customer and the market.

Who are my customers?

How you define your business will help answer this question. The consumer—the ultimate user of a product/service—is always the customer. In most cases, we have two customers—external and internal (employees). For each, wants and needs must be satisfied for a positive outcome.

What does my customer value?

This may be the most important question, yet it is often overlooked because we assume we know the answer. We need to remember the customer never buys a product; the customer buys the satisfaction of a want. Bottom line—customers *buy value.*

Never lose sight of the importance of staying connected to your customers, asking questions, listening, and making sure you continue to deliver value.

TODAY, I WILL TAKE STOCK OF WHAT BUSINESS I'M IN BY ASSESSING
THE FOLLOWING:

WHAT MARKET AM I IN, AND WHAT CUSTOMER NEEDS AND WANTS DOES
MY BUSINESS SATISFY?

_____

_____

_____

_____

WHAT VALUE ARE MY EXTERNAL CUSTOMERS BUYING FROM ME?

_____

_____

_____

_____

WHAT VALUE DO MY EMPLOYEES SEEK BY WORKING WITH ME?

_____

_____

_____

_____

I WILL EVALUATE THIS BECAUSE:

_____

_____

_____

Visioning

Without a compelling vision and clear goals, your leadership really doesn't matter, because leadership is about going somewhere.

Ken Blanchard, author, speaker, and business consultant

Crafting a vision is probably the single most important role of a leader.

If we are like Alice in Wonderland asking the Cheshire Cat for general directions, and we cannot say where we want to go, then it will not matter much which way we choose.

Vision begins and ends with your heart. You've got to be able to feel it before you can see it and, as a leader, you need to see it before others can.

In "The Power of Vision," from *Leading from a Higher Level,* Jesse Stoner, Ken Blanchard, and Drea Zigarmi identify three key elements of a compelling vision. Every vision should have:

- A significant purpose: What business are you in?
- A picture of the future: Where are we going?
- Clear values: How do we guide behavior and make decisions?

A vision is not something drafted and set aside. It needs to be a daily guide for action. It needs to be simple, and it should connect with people and empower them. It has energy in and of itself. It is a state of being; it is what could be, it is what will be. When members of your organization are convinced that tomorrow will be better than today, morale improves and hope abounds. This results in an energy that drives the mission and helps maintain an optimism, which translates into, "We will do this. We will get there."

If you are a student of history, consider which leaders had vision and could communicate it well—and which could not. History offers examples of both.

Now, go back to your vision. Ask yourself, "Do I feel it? Can I see it? Does it have a significant purpose? Does it tell people where we're going? And does it illustrate clear values that guide our decisions and behavior day in and day out?" If not...journal this.

*T*ODAY, I COMMIT TO FEELING MY VISION FOR MY TEAM AND MAKING THE TIME TO ELABORATE IT FOR MYSELF FIRST, THEN FOR OTHERS.

I WILL SHARE MY VISION WITH:

_____

_____

_____

_____

_____

HERE'S HOW I'LL SHARE MY VISION:

_____

_____

_____

_____

_____

AND HERE IS WHY I'LL SHARE MY VISION:

_____

_____

_____

_____

_____

_____

Crafting the Vision
and Sharing It

Vision without a task is only a dream. A task without a vision is but drudgery.
But vision with a task is a dream fulfilled.

Anonymous

An online search brings up thousands of resources on how to craft the perfect vision statement. Once you have explored your vision, it's time to craft it—put it into words—and share it and get buy-in.

Here are some keys:

Make it clear, concise, and easy to communicate. Don't draft a nine-page vision statement and expect your team to jump for joy and your customers to rave. Articulate your vision in a few short sentences.

Involve key members of your team. Bringing too many people into the process can lead to confusion and compromise core principles. Your key members can lead on sharing the vision and ensuring that others can see and feel the vision and invest in it.

Expect resistance. A bold vision scares those who feel entitled and comfortable and sometimes their resistance comes coded; they may not directly approach you, but may do subtle things that undermine and sabotage your efforts. Stay connected, listen, be aware of what's going on.

If you have prepared yourself—if you have earned your team's trust thanks to your character and your competence—it will be easier to take the vision from "me" to "we." To do this, you need to be in tune with the aspirations and goals of your people.

TODAY, I WILL SET A TIME TO MEET WITH KEY TEAM MEMBERS TO CAST A VISION. ONCE I HAVE THE TIME SET, I WILL DRAFT SOME SAMPLE VISIONS.

I WILL DO THIS BY:

_____

_____

_____

_____

_____

_____

_____

_____

AND THIS IS WHY I WILL DO THIS AND DO IT THIS WAY:

_____

_____

_____

_____

_____

_____

_____

We think, each of us, that we're much more rational than we are. And we think
that we make our decisions because we have good reasons to make them.
Even when it's the other way around. We believe in the reasons, because we've
already made the decision.

Daniel Kahneman, psychologist and 2002 Nobel Laureate for Economics

We make decisions all day long. Some are more important than others. Some are "mission critical" and have serious consequences. Whatever the case or circumstance may be, consequences accompany every decision. I've learned that the decisions I make today will determine the stories I tell tomorrow.

Certainly, our gut and intuition have a role in decision-making. However, gut and intuition are typically based on our past experiences. That is fine; we just need to be careful about too much emotion clouding our decision-making. Let's remember: the emotion of anger is the most prominent emotion that, not consciously expressed, impairs good judgment.

The following are some guidelines I use in decision-making. They are basic, but helpful:

◦ Maintain a vision of the big picture.
◦ Gather all relevant information.
◦ Listen to those closest to the situation.
◦ Narrow the options to the best.
◦ Examine the likely outcome from each option.

Make the decision based on the following:

◦ Is it in alignment with the mission?
◦ How does the decision affect all stakeholders?

Being decisive is critical for every leader. Wishy-washy leadership will not sustain relationships or processes—whether with team members or clients.

Today, I will examine my decision-making acumen. I will do this by answering these questions:

WHERE AM I FINDING IT DIFFICULT TO MAKE DECISIONS?

_____

_____

_____

_____

HOW DOES THIS DIFFICULTY UNFOLD?

_____

_____

_____

_____

IS IT BECAUSE I AM MISSING SOME OF THE STEPS LISTED ABOVE?
IF SO, WHICH ONES AND WHAT DO I NEED TO DO DIFFERENTLY?

_____

_____

_____

_____

I WILL DO THIS BECAUSE:

_____

_____

_____

What Your People Expect

Expectation. That is the true soul of art. If you can give a man more than he expects, then he will laud you his entire life. If you can create an air of anticipation and feed it properly, you will succeed.

Brandon Sanderson, author

One responsibility of a leader is to create expectations for our team members. Failure to do so may cause several issues and consequences.

However, I have a challenge for you: How about role reversal? That is, "What do your people expect from you?"

They may not express these to you outright, but the following are what I have learned people expect from their leader:

- To communicate openly, honestly, and frequently
- To be predictable and consistent
- To have a plan for their growth
- To exhibit self-confidence balanced with humility
- To encourage them (Remember: you need to be the Chief Encouragement Officer)
- To challenge them
- To let them know how they are doing
- To always praise when appropriate
- To be decisive and fair
- To inform them of changes that will affect them

I am sure there are many more expectations, but these are some that come to my mind. I find it helpful from time to time to conduct a self-assessment on how I am doing with each of these.

TODAY, I WILL RATE MYSELF ON HOW WELL I AM FULFILLING MY TEAM'S
EXPECTATIONS OF ME.

I WILL DO THIS BY CHOOSING FIVE AREAS, RATING MYSELF ON A SCALE OF 1 TO 10,
10 BEING THE BEST. THEN I WILL RANK THOSE FIVE AND CHOOSE THE TOP
THREE AND PUT IN PLACE A PLAN TO "MOVE THE NEEDLE" A COUPLE OF DEGREES.

HERE ARE MY TOP THREE IN NEED OF IMPROVEMENT:

_____

_____

_____

TODAY, I COMMIT TO WORKING ON THIS AREA OF IMPROVEMENT:

_____

_____

_____

_____

I WILL DO THIS BY:

_____

_____

_____

I WILL DO THIS BECAUSE:

_____

_____

_____

Mindset

Life's most persistent and urgent question is, what are you doing for others?

Martin Luther King, Jr., civil rights leader, orator, and Nobel Peace Prize Laureate

"Servant leadership." Volumes have been written on the subject and, like many subjects about leading, first there is resistance—I certainly balked at the word "servant." Then follows embracing the idea. But, if we are not vigilant, it becomes easy to forget. But servant leadership can be the mindset we bring to our role as leaders—an "others first" mindset.

Years ago, I conflated servant leadership with servitude, and I imagined an activity performed by a relatively low-skilled person. My "old school" mindset assumed that if we serve, people will have a lesser view of us. Yet, over the years, I have come to see that could not be further from the truth.

Before you fall into the same trap I did, consider mothers. They naturally serve their family members and likely are the ones who have served us more than anyone else. So, the question is: "Do you have a lesser view of mothers—or a higher one?" Most everyone would say higher. Why is that?

Serving others has the opposite effect on them of what we think. People are drawn to those who connect with them, who add value to their lives, and who serve them.

The mindset of servant leadership is not about position or skill; it's about seeking and finding ways to add value.

Part of servant leadership is the belief that people are our most important asset. Possessing a leader mindset means desiring improvement and constantly moving in that direction, which influences and encourages others to do the same.

Consider the following: What is your attitude toward servant leadership? In what ways can you see yourself adding value to those around you? Journal about the first question and jot down some ideas in response to the second. Then, plan your day with these in mind.

TODAY, I WILL COMMIT TO SEEING OPPORTUNITIES WHERE I CAN SERVE OTHERS, AND I WILL MAKE NOTE OF THEM.

A PERSON I WILL SERVE TODAY IS:

_____

HERE'S HOW I WILL DO THAT:

_____

_____

_____

_____

_____

_____

_____

_____

HERE'S WHY I'LL DO THAT:

_____

_____

_____

_____

_____

_____

_____

The Currency of Relationships

Trust is the glue of life. It's the most essential ingredient in effective communication. It's the foundational principle that holds all relationships.

Stephen R. Covey, educator, author, and businessman

Picture an employee with a thought bubble. Inside the bubble, the person is thinking, "Can I trust you?"

The employer/leader picks up on this and says aloud, "Are you kidding?! Of course you can trust me; I'm your leader."

History books are filled with examples of fallen leaders. They fell simply because they breached the trust of the people. Is it any wonder people have deep concerns about leaders in whom they place their trust?

Trust is not just about trustworthiness or honesty. It also relates to competency. A trustworthy automotive technician will never try to snooker you into getting a repair you don't need, but do they actually repair what is needed?

Trust encompasses caring *and* competency. As a leader, you need both. Trust comes from matching your walk with your talk. Competency comes from understanding where you need to improve and working on that, perhaps as part of lifelong learning.

Some years ago, Gallup conducted an international study where workers were surveyed about trust, and 58 percent said they trust a stranger more than their boss. That stings! What leader does not want to be trusted in the workplace? After all, if we have no trust, there is no relationship. Trust is the currency of every relationship.

This is what I have learned to be true:

- Trust rules your personal credibility.
- Trust rules your team's cohesiveness.
- Trust rules your ability to get things done.
- Trust rules your organization's innovation and performance.
- Trust rules your brand image.
- Trust rules just about everything you do.

Getting people to work together begins with building mutual trust. Before asking for trust from others, you must demonstrate trust in them. That may require vulnerability on your part. Share your values, wants, hopes, and what you are willing and not willing to do. As leaders, we need to be consistent in our actions as well as candid, forthright, and clear in our communications.

This may be a good time to test our trust meter. Let's remember: trust rules.

*T*ODAY, I WILL DEMONSTRATE MY TRUST IN:

_____

I WILL DO THIS BY:

_____

_____

_____

_____

_____

_____

_____

I WILL DO THIS BECAUSE:

_____

_____

_____

_____

_____

_____

_____

What You'll
Receive as a Leader

In the end, as a leader, you are always going to get a combination of two things: what you create and what you allow.

Dr. Henry Cloud, psychologist, leadership expert, and author

As leaders, we wear many hats. After all, the buck stops…well, you know where.

Once, I had a conversation with a young man who had just graduated from high school. He asked about the leader's role. Not so much the day-to-day functions, but "big picture" (his words).

I described, as best as I could, the "big picture" for him: Leaders are people developers, change agents, decision makers, problem solvers, visionaries, culture protectors, strategy developers, coaches, communicators, talent recruiters, conflict managers, team builders and…I'll stop there.

He said to me, "Wow, there is a ton of things you have to do."

The leader's plate overflows with responsibilities. Two things increase or decrease this, and these are two things that will always guide what you end up getting, in terms of positive results or further problems. The two things are what you create and what you allow.

Think about that for a moment. Is that true in your world? It certainly has been true in mine. As you ponder that thought, I have two more questions for you: Is what you have created what you really want? And are you allowing—tolerating—something you should not?

TODAY, WHAT IS ONE THING I AM CREATING WHICH SHOULD LEAD TO
POSITIVE RESULTS?

_____

_____

_____

AND WHAT IS ONE THING I AM ALLOWING/TOLERATING WHICH WILL
LEAD TO FURTHER PROBLEMS?

_____

_____

_____

I WILL CREATE MORE OF WHAT I WANT BY:

_____

_____

_____

BECAUSE IT DOES NOT SERVE US, I WILL DISALLOW:

_____

_____

_____

I WILL DO THIS BECAUSE:

_____

_____

Are You an
Authentic Leader?

Fear of being shamed causes people to put on masks and live in fear and pretense, creating a stronghold of pride. Authentic, transparent leaders encourage people to develop trust through their own honesty and vulnerability. They do not view transparency as weakness, but recognize it as a source of their virtue, power, and anointing, because power flows through humility.

Laura Gagnon, author

A good question to ask ourselves from time to time is, "Am I truly an authentic leader?" Authentic may sound cliché, but it's critical to maintain authenticity if we want to lead people, and what authenticity boils down to is, are your feet and your mouth going in the same direction?

This begins with living our values. What we truly care about—not just talk about—and living by that code daily is the beginning of being an authentic leader.

I believe our people deserve a leader who is true to what matters most. When we pursue our purpose, we are demonstrating our authenticity.

Most of us have mission statements or purpose statements, and they are likely in writing and prominently displayed in an office or conference room. A display serves as a strong reminder. But what is more important is having your people see you actually living your values and purpose.

Whether you're building a new team or leading an established, seasoned group, the power to attract is priceless. People join people. Sure, the brand may have some appeal, but inevitably it's the discussions and experiences they've had while spending time with you and your team that makes them decide to join you.

You need to know why someone would join your organization. What is it about you—and your organization—that is attractive? Are you communicating your personal values statement? Your organization's mission statement? Are your interactions authentic and your delivery purposeful? Does your team see you as authentic so that they can speak with conviction when representing your organization? In this period of reflection, spend some time evaluating your actions. Are you living your values and purpose?

$\mathcal{T}$ODAY, I WILL MAKE TIME TO CONTEMPLATE MY AUTHENTICITY AS A LEADER. I WILL DO THIS BY ANSWERING THE QUESTIONS: WHERE DO I EXCEL IN THIS AND WHERE DO I FALL SHORT? I WILL GIVE AT LEAST THREE EXAMPLES OF EACH.

_____

_____

_____

_____

_____

_____

IN THE AREAS WHERE I FALL SHORT, HOW CAN I CHANGE MY APPROACH TO BECOME MORE AUTHENTIC?

_____

_____

_____

_____

_____

I WILL DO THIS BECAUSE:

_____

_____

_____

_____

Timeless Truths

If you learn from defeat, you haven't really lost.

Zig Ziglar, motivational speaker

Over the last couple of years, reflection has become a key part of daily life for many. It could be the tumultuous times we're in, aging, or a combination of both (likely both, in my case).

Below are some truths I have learned over the years to help during challenging times:

- Start each day with a renewed commitment to be passionate about your leadership role. Leadership is a privilege, not a right. It's a responsibility, a way of life—not a title.
- The first person you lead is yourself. We are responsible for our character, our competence and our courage. We can't delegate those responsibilities to anyone else, nor can we blame anyone other than ourselves when we fall short.
- Be in love with what you do and the people you serve and lead. Your people know when you are genuine and authentic.
- Accept failure. We know it is "part of the game." Don't be afraid of failure—it's not permanent. There is always a lesson.
- Be aware of your communication cues: non-verbal, verbal and written. Listening is more important than talking. Lead with your body language and tone. Remember, a smile is priceless.

$\mathcal{T}$ODAY, I WILL ASSESS MYSELF ON THE FOLLOWING: HOW DO I VIEW LEADERSHIP IN GENERAL—MINE IN PARTICULAR, ESPECIALLY IN THE AREAS OF CHARACTER, COMPETENCE AND COURAGE?

_____

_____

_____

_____

AM I TRULY IN LOVE WITH WHAT I AM DOING? IF I AM, CAN PEOPLE FEEL MY AUTHENTIC PASSION? IF NOT, WHAT DO I NEED TO DO?

_____

_____

_____

_____

HOW ARE MY SPOKEN AND WRITTEN COMMUNICATION CUES—TONE, GESTURES? HOW WELL IS IT RECEIVED? HOW WELL AM I LISTENING?

_____

_____

_____

I WILL EVALUATE THE WAY I AM LEADING BECAUSE:

_____

_____

_____

Good Students, Great Coaching Leaders

Learners are not always leaders, but leaders are always learners.

Anonymous

As leaders, we face the danger of the status quo. We focus on supporting and developing our team, growing our business, and, in today's environment, we're learning new ways to manage, lead, and drive results remotely. Amid these demands, it's easy to neglect our own personal growth and development.

As good leaders, we recognize it is not only about investing in others; it's also about investing in ourselves. What I have learned is, when you grow first, you're in a much better position to help others grow.

Throughout my career, I've learned that we must remain eager to learn: We must be on a journey of lifetime growth. A mentor asked me this simple question, "When was the last time you did something for the first time?" Read that again: When was the last time you did something for the first time? Powerful question, right?

When we give ourselves permission to make our own personal growth a priority, we create more value for those around us. Here is a simple formula for why we should keep growing:

- Who we are is dictated by our growth.
- Who we are determines who we attract.
- Who we attract defines the success of our team.

What can you do today that will help you tomorrow?

*T*ODAY, I WILL FOCUS ON MY EAGERNESS TO LEARN. WHERE HAVE I BEEN
SLIPPING INTO THE GRIND OF THE STATUS QUO?

_____

_____

_____

WHERE AND HOW DO I NEED TO STOP NEGLECTING MY OWN LEARNING AND
GET MORE INTENTIONAL ABOUT LEARNING NEW THINGS?

_____

_____

_____

WHEN WAS THE LAST TIME I DID SOMETHING FOR THE FIRST TIME?
HOW DID THAT FEEL? AND WHERE DID IT LEAD?

_____

_____

_____

HOW WILL I BECOME MORE INTENTIONAL ABOUT MY OWN LEARNING? WILL I SIGN
UP FOR AN ONLINE COURSE? ATTEND AN IN-PERSON WORKSHOP? REACH OUT
TO SOMEONE WHOSE LEADERSHIP I ADMIRE AND HAVE A CONVERSATION?

_____

_____

I WILL DO ALL OF THIS BECAUSE:

_____

_____

We Have Adversity. Now, What?

Every setback is a set-up for the comeback.

Jack Welch, CEO, General Electric, 1981–2001

Businesses are composed of people and so, as with people, businesses will always face difficult and challenging times to one degree or another. For the most part, external factors—supply-chain issues, labor shortages, proposed mandates and more—lie beyond our control. No one wants to make light of these, but as leaders, we are not supposed to have it easy, and it's our job to grow from these circumstances.

Equally serious as any current state of affairs, if not more so, is our mindset and behavior. Often, leadership is best learned and honed through adversity. I like to refer to setbacks as "the classroom of the comeback." We must learn how to translate what we discovered in the "classroom" to become an even better leader.

As leaders, we own the comeback. It is our job to re-examine our systems, our operations, our team members, and our strategy: What needs to be altered?

We are the change agents, and there is no better time than the present to see what we can do differently to ensure we're doing right by our people, company, and clients.

TODAY, I WILL TAKE A DEEP DIVE ON OUR PEOPLE, PROCESSES, OR CLIENTS. I'LL DO THIS BY:

_____

_____

_____

_____

_____

_____

_____

AND THIS IS WHY I'LL DO THIS:

_____

_____

_____

_____

AMONG PEOPLE, PROCESSES, AND CLIENTS, WHICH IS MOST IN NEED OF MY ATTENTION? HERE'S HOW I'LL APPLY MY ATTENTION:

_____

_____

_____

_____

_____

Gratitude

Cultivate the habit of being grateful for every good thing that comes to you, and to give thanks continuously. And because all things have contributed to your advancement, you should include all things in your gratitude.

Ralph Waldo Emerson, essayist, poet, philosopher, and abolitionist

Part of preparation is preparing one's heart for gratitude. It involves a kind of space-clearing, a recognition that whatever success comes our way, we are not—we are never—self-made. No one person can do it alone.

In my case, I started a business with borrowed money in my living room with no business address. Whatever success I may have is because of God-given gifts and plenty of other people who poured themselves into me. Many people—parents, teachers, coaches, pastors, business people and scores of others—influenced me. There simply is no "self-made."

Preparing one's heart for gratitude is simple: It means you cultivate gratitude. Every night, I do the "FOG" test before I sleep. I think back through the day and ask myself: Who and what helped me to feel fulfilled, optimistic and grateful? (I choose three of those people and I give thanks for them.) Where did I add value to someone? And, what was one positive thing that happened today? This is the perfect set-up for tomorrow.

This is a habit for every leader and would-be leader. And it does not require much—just recalling who and what helped create fulfillment, optimism, and gratitude in our lives.

Find a time you can do this every day. See how it changes your life. I also suggest you let people know when they do things that create fulfillment and optimism, and when they do things that inspire gratitude in you.

TODAY, I WILL BE SURE TO THANK:

_____

I WILL THANK THIS INDIVIDUAL FOR:

_____

_____

_____

_____

_____

I WILL DO THIS IN THIS MANNER:

_____

_____

_____

_____

AND I WILL DO THIS BECAUSE:

_____

_____

_____

_____

The Daily Five

The concept is each day be intentional on achieving each of these actions.
When I do, I am fulfilled, optimistic and grateful—*my masterpiece.*
I would challenge you to identify five and seek to accomplish each one every day.
Most days, I am successful at four or all five. It is all about being intentional.

GOD TIME
Read and pray before the start of each day.

CREATE
Write, plan, strategize, think.

ADD VALUE
Coach, connect (in person, phone, text), communicate, teach.

REFLECT
Journal. What happened? What did I learn? Sleep on positives.

FORWARD
My main event for tomorrow, my #1 priority where I must be all in.

CHAPTER TWO

Cultivating Connection

We live in an age of unprecedented connectivity with others—from phone and text to video, social media, chat apps, e-mail, and snail mail. Yet, paradoxically, the time we live in may as well be called "The Age of Disconnection" because, for the most part, despite the near ubiquity, speed, and convenience of these means of communication, none compares with connecting in-person where we have the opportunity to get tone of voice and inflection, body language, and, most important of all, eye contact.

Connectivity does not equal connection. Connecting requires leaders to recognize the need for, tap into, and develop many "soft" skills—those intangible traits and habits that are the glue that holds our masterpieces together. There is no way we can lead others without first connecting with them. And that is what this section is all about—how we can hone our ability to connect.

Today, connecting is more important than ever as each person has the capacity to take on more and different roles or affiliate with more diverse groups. Connecting may lead us toward a kind of social fragmentation while also helping to propel us to celebrate *and* bridge differences. Whether you lead a corporate team or you lead your family, the principles of connecting are the same: It's all about empathy, which is the ability to put ourselves in others' shoes and connect on an emotional level.

The events of 2020 and 2021 will probably have spawned many opportunities to connect with others and certainly will have shown us why the skills involved in connecting are priceless.

The entries that follow give you plenty of occasions to practice empathy and enhance your connection skills.

Everyone Is
Someone's CEO

I consider my ability to arouse enthusiasm among men the greatest asset I possess.
The way to develop the best that is in a man is by appreciation and encouragement.

Charles M. Schwab, steel magnate

You may not be the chief executive officer or the chief information officer of the company where you work, but you may very well be someone's—maybe many someones'—CEO and CIO or chief encouragement officer and chief inspiration officer. A hallmark of leading others is influencing them. And what does it mean to influence, if not to inspire and to encourage—literally, to breathe into and to pour courage into?

As leaders, our days are filled with opportunities to encourage and inspire. Are we taking advantage of them? If we aren't, we are letting good things pass us by.

$\mathcal{T}$ODAY, I WILL CONSIDER WHETHER AND TO WHAT EXTENT I AM FULFILLING
MY ROLES AS CHIEF ENCOURAGEMENT OFFICER AND CHIEF INSPIRATION OFFICER.
HOW WELL AM I DOING IN THIS? WHAT CAN I DO TO IMPROVE?

_____

_____

_____

_____

_____

_____

IS THERE ANYONE IN PARTICULAR ON MY TEAM WHO COULD BENEFIT FROM
MY ENCOURAGEMENT? FOR THAT PERSON, TODAY I WILL:

_____

_____

_____

_____

_____

I WILL DO THIS BECAUSE:

_____

_____

_____

_____

A Contact Sport

People don't care how much you know until they know how much you care.

Theodore Roosevelt, 26th U.S. President

Emotional and social intelligence guru Daniel Goleman identified empathy as an attribute of emotional intelligence. Empathy is the capacity to understand or feel what another person is experiencing within their frame of reference. In other words, it's the capacity to place oneself in another person's position.

If we're not willing to focus, listen and connect on an emotional level, we will not develop empathy. The more we get out and make contact, the more we develop and evolve our empathetic responses. After all, *leadership is a contact sport.*

There simply is no substitute for interacting deeply with the people you lead. I have learned that people are looking for a leader who first understands and then helps according to that knowledge.

Some helpful empathy keys are:

○ Focus on active listening. When asking questions, actually listen: Keep your eyes on the other person at all times; when they stop talking, count to five before you respond because they may have more to say.

○ Ask yourself, "Am I taking the time to really understand?"

○ Ask yourself, "Am I sensitive, compassionate, and caring toward the people I lead?"

TODAY, I WILL CHOOSE ONE PERSON WITH WHOM I CAN PRACTICE EMPATHY.
FIRST, I WILL ASK MYSELF WHAT I KNOW ABOUT THIS PERSON, AND THEN I WILL
SEEK TO LEARN MORE. I WILL DO THIS BY PRACTICING ACTIVE LISTENING
AND I WILL MAKE THE TIME TO UNDERSTAND.

_____

_____

_____

_____

_____

_____

_____

_____

_____

_____

AND I WILL DO THIS BECAUSE:

_____

_____

_____

_____

The Example?

Example is not the main thing in influencing others. It is the only thing.

Albert Schweitzer, theologian, organist, author, and physician/surgeon

What Dr. Schweitzer was really saying was that all the words we speak as leaders mean nothing if our lives don't back up the words. Being credible is a critical quality for any leader to possess. Hypocrisy murders credibility. The late U.S. Secretary of State General Colin Powell put it more specifically: "You can issue all the memos and give all the motivational speeches you want, but if the people in your organization don't see you putting forth your very best every single day, they won't either."

Most people are visual learners, and this applies to leadership, as well. People need to see an example or model before they really understand.

Of course, the words we use to communicate are important. Good communication enhances clarity. But good modeling brings to life what we are communicating. The most valuable gift we can give others is a good example; leadership is more caught than taught.

A professional staffing company conducted a survey of employees to find what was the single most important trait they wanted in their supervisor. The resounding response? They wanted their leader to lead by example.

In the end, communication that transforms combines clear speech and consistent modeling.

Today, I WILL BE INTENTIONAL IN OBSERVING HOW I SPEAK AND HOW I MODEL BEHAVIOR FOR OTHERS. I WILL CHECK TO SEE WHETHER MY WORD AND MY DEED ARE IN ALIGNMENT.

I WILL DO THIS WITH:

_____

_____

_____

I WILL DO THIS BY:

_____

_____

_____

_____

_____

_____

_____

AND I WILL DO THIS BECAUSE:

_____

_____

_____

AT THE END OF THE DAY TODAY OR EARLY TOMORROW BEFORE I START MY DAY, I WILL CHECK IN WITH MYSELF TO SEE HOW I DID.

The Supporting Cast

Every great athlete, artist and aspiring being has a great team to help them flourish and succeed—personally and professionally. Even the so-called "solo star" has a strong supporting cast helping them shine, thrive, and take flight.

Rasheed Ogunlaru, life coach and motivational speaker

Everyone has a story. My mentor, John Maxwell, talks about a book given to him by one of his mentors called, *The Greatest Story Ever Told.* The book had only blank pages. John's mentor instructed him to fill the pages with intentionality.

It is true—we all have a story. We play a critical role in the story of the people we choose to lead. As leaders, we are members of the supporting cast in the lives of the people we lead, and we need to remember it is always their story, not ours. We need to connect and support their dreams. Those we lead need to see and feel that we believe in them—and that we are committed to helping them become all they dream to be.

People have a better chance of growing and developing when those closest to them believe in them. It is our job to help them be in the spotlight. As cast members, we must support the star.

$\mathcal{T}$ODAY, AS A MEMBER OF THEIR SUPPORTING CAST, I WILL BE INTENTIONAL
IN THE LIVES OF (THREE PEOPLE):

_____

_____

_____

I WILL DO THIS BY:

_____

_____

_____

_____

_____

_____

_____

AND I WILL DO THIS BECAUSE:

_____

_____

_____

_____

_____

_____

Three Things Your People Want to Know

I worry that business leaders are more interested in material gain than they are in having the patience to build up a strong organization, and a strong organization starts with caring for their people.

John Wooden, legendary basketball coach

We all know that one critical aspect of building a productive team is the selection of the right talent. Once you believe you have the right person for the opportunity, that person intuitively has three questions they want answered. Keep in mind they may not ask these questions directly, but, deep down, the answers may be deal breakers. They are looking for you to answer with your actions. The last thing you want is to have the person at risk of walking, especially when you have invested time to identify the right person for the job.

The three questions are:

Do you care about me?

The challenge here for most leaders is how to sincerely demonstrate care. You have to get intentional about what I call "Cry-Sing-Dream." Ask yourself, "Do I really know this person? Do I know their pain (what makes them cry)? Do I know what puts a spring in their step (what makes them sing)? Do I know what they most long for (their dream)? Have I connected with them on an emotional level?" When you are one to one with them, are you doing more talking than listening? You demonstrate care best when they see you are "all in" on them. When you are with them, make them feel that they are the most important person in your world.

Can I trust you?

As leaders, we must be consistent in our behavior. I like to say, "I must be predictable." We break others' trust when our walk doesn't match our talk. Remember—trust is the currency for a relationship. It is also the currency in leadership—no trust, no leadership—plain and simple. Ask yourself, "Do I follow through consistently? Am I communicating effectively?"

How will you help me?

If you have selected the right person, trust me—they want to grow personally and professionally. Employees expect their leader to provide the tools, resources, and opportunities to grow. Leaders must create an environment for growth—programs, resources, and recognition, as well as challenging them to new heights.

I realize we can't connect with all our people at this level. However, every person on the leadership team must be responsible for developing another team member. Remember—team members are waiting for the answers to the three questions.

$\mathcal{T}$ODAY, I WILL REFLECT ON HOW MY TOP TEAM MEMBERS MAY BE ASKING ME ABOUT CARE, TRUST, AND HELP AND HOW I WOULD LIKE TO ANSWER THEM.

_____

_____

_____

_____

_____

_____

_____

_____

_____

_____

I WILL DO THIS BECAUSE:

_____

_____

_____

_____

_____

The Warm and Fuzzy
of a Productive Environment

Never underestimate the power of the personal touch.

Tom Peters, business expert and author

As leaders, we strive to maintain a productive environment—one that provides growth opportunities, challenges, recognition and encouragement. Certainly, these are characteristics of a productive growth-oriented organization. Studies have shown that people are generally 15 percent logical and 85 percent emotional. Unlike machines, which are easier to understand because they typically operate in predictable, predetermined ways, people have emotions, feelings, and internal beliefs that trigger responses and motivate behavior.

We live in a logical, linear, need-to-measure world. As leaders, we are naturally results oriented and we'd like for everything to be logical, linear and conducted on a need-to-measure basis. It is easy from that perspective to dismiss the 85 percent warm and fuzzy, soft stuff. Yet, we can be blinded by the power of that "soft stuff" in developing and coaching people.

I have learned that leaders influence productivity in three ways and to the degree or extent that:

- *You* sincerely believe that team members can achieve higher performance.
- *Team members* believe that *you* believe that.
- There is mutual trust and respect between you and them.

As a leader, you play a critical role in influencing productivity and you need to pay attention to how you exercise your "soft skills" and how well you stay connected to your people—in particular, your best people. Soft skills are not "kumbaya"; rather, leaders need to be likable for a sustained period in order for someone to follow them.

*T*ODAY, I WILL FOCUS ON HOW I STAY CONNECTED TO MY PEOPLE, ESPECIALLY
MY BEST PEOPLE. I WILL DO THIS BY:

_____

_____

_____

_____

_____

_____

_____

_____

_____

_____

_____

I WILL DO THIS BECAUSE:

_____

_____

_____

_____

_____

_____

Don't Just Act Interested —Be Interested

Everyone has an invisible sign hanging over their neck saying, "Make me feel important."

Mary Kay Ash, founder, Mary Kay Cosmetics, Inc.

I love this quote from Mary Kay Ash. Because leaders have the responsibility of developing their people, listening and being sincerely interested is a critical skill. I am not sure we can ever perfect it, but I know there is no substitute for practice, practice, practice.

There is an old joke that says, "You can't fake sincerity." In my opinion, you can't fake interest, either, so save your energy and don't even try. The more you want to influence and get through to your people, the more sincere your interest in them needs to be.

How do you improve the skill of being interested while being sincere when you do it? I have learned the first key is to stop thinking of a conversation as a tennis match: she scored a point, now it's my turn.

Instead, think of it as a detective game. Your goal is to learn as much about the other person as you can. Go into the conversation with the expectation of learning. Believe me, this will become evident in your eyes and body language. They will feel your interest. Allow them to tell the story. Often, we are tempted to jump in as soon as we can—do everything you can to avoid this.

Do your homework. Come prepared with questions that demonstrate genuine interest. In a business setting, I've found questions that begin with "What, how, tell me more, what would it mean?" can be effective. Remember, you're building an organization of people. People need to know that you care, that you're interested in what they're saying and how they're doing, and that you're invested in them.

TODAY, I WILL PRACTICE CONNECTING WITH A PERSON IN WHOM I AM
SINCERELY INTERESTED. I WILL DO THIS BY:

_____

_____

_____

_____

_____

_____

_____

_____

_____

_____

I WILL DO THIS BECAUSE:

_____

_____

_____

_____

_____

Strengthen Others

When you give people a choice about being a part of what's happening, they're more likely to be committed to a project. Is there a piece of something you are working on that you could open up to others?

James M. Kouzes and Barry Z. Posner, authors

Creating a climate in which people are fully engaged and feel in control of their own lives is at the heart of strengthening others.

When we enable people to take ownership of and responsibility for their group's success, we enhance their competence and confidence in their abilities. When we listen to their ideas, involve them in important decisions, and acknowledge and give credit for their contributions, we foster empowerment through the organization.

Leadership experts and authors James Kouzes and Barry Posner refer to the Power Paradox in *The Leadership Challenge: How to Make Extraordinary Things Happen in Organizations.* They believe that when you replace the old style of leadership of employing force with empathy and modesty, you live in the Power Paradox. You empower others by publicly expressing confidence in them.

Over the years, I have heard from people whose leaders empowered them. They told me things like, "I was able to make decisions about key aspects of the project." And, "All the financial data was shared with me." Or, "I was able to exercise my discretion about how we handle a delicate situation." My favorite was, "My manager publicly expressed confidence in my ability to handle the assignment," demonstrating both encouragement and trust.

These are examples of what empowering others means. The bottom line is, feeling powerful —literally, feeling able—comes from a deep sense of being in control of your own life. We all share this fundamental need. We just need to remember that the more empowered our team members feel, the stronger our team will be and the greater the impact our organization will make on the people it serves.

TODAY, I WILL EXAMINE WHERE I CAN OPEN UP AVENUES TO EMPOWER MEMBERS
OF MY TEAM—AT HOME, AT WORK, AT AN ORGANIZATION WHERE I VOLUNTEER.
I WILL CHOOSE A PERSON IN THESE AREAS I CAN EMPOWER BY:

_____

_____

_____

_____

_____

_____

_____

_____

_____

I WILL DO THIS BECAUSE:

_____

_____

_____

_____

_____

The Importance
of Being Sensitive

The sensitivity of men to small matters, and their indifference to great ones,
indicates a strange inversion.

Blaise Pascal, mathematician, physicist, and religious philosopher

We live in a time of paradoxes, where "being sensitive" all too often translates into taking offense at things we have perhaps misinterpreted. Yet, at the same time, we seem to lack developing our own sensitivity to the needs of other people. So, when I highlight the importance of being sensitive as a way to connect with others, it is the latter I am talking about.

The ability to work with people is important; understanding people is critical.

Over the years, I have realized some beliefs about people that have proven helpful in the process of developing them and their leadership. Below are some of these:

- People have untapped potential which, when discovered, can help them to significantly increase their productivity.
- People produce more when their leaders respect them and expect the best from them.
- People will generally produce more when they feel the role they play (their job), has meaning and they are valued in the big picture.
- People generally want to do the right thing, a feel-good thing.
- When you express a positive belief in people, it is likely to produce a reciprocity—they'll want to do their best for you.
- Listen to people without biases—not always toward agreement, but simply valuing them as a person.
- Take on the role of the other person: How do they see things versus how I see things? (This is empathy, walking in their shoes.)
- Listen with your eyes and feelings—not to just their words, but their tone, gestures, body language, and their energy.

The bottom line is, your people are thinking, "If you don't understand me, how can you lead me?"

$\mathcal{T}$ODAY, I WILL MAKE THE TIME TO PRACTICE A HIGH LEVEL OF SENSITIVITY
TOWARD A MEMBER OF MY TEAM:

_____

I WILL DO THIS BY:

_____

_____

_____

_____

_____

I WILL DO THIS BECAUSE:

_____

_____

_____

_____

_____

AND WITH WHAT I LEARN, I WILL:

_____

_____

_____

_____

_____

Knowledge vs Caring

The number one productivity problem today is the leader is out of touch with his/her people.

Tom Peters, business expert and author

As leaders, we have got to initiate connection. Heart first, then head. Our people, especially our key people, must feel the care. We can say we care all we want, but how do we show it? And how do our people experience our caring?

I have learned to start by asking myself, "What three non-business things do I know about this person?" We might ask: Do they have a dog? What kinds of activities are their children involved in? What was their first job?

An example of this hit home some years ago when I showed up at the piano recital of the daughter of one of my key people. This person was one of our leading sales reps. He was blown away. After thanking me for being there, he later came up to me and asked how I knew about his daughter's piano lessons and when and where the recital was. I responded simply that I had heard him speak about her and I did a little research and I wanted to experience his joy and pride for her accomplishments.

It turned out, the entire event taught him something about coaching. He realized he should pay more attention to his better clients and listen more about what was important in their lives.

This also points to the importance of listening, and listening well, as part of the care we bring to the people we work with, the people we serve.

Consider the difference between the extent of your knowledge and the extent of your caring. Regarding one or two key people, ask yourself what you really know about them outside of work and how you might help them get what they would like.

TODAY, I WILL COMMIT TO HELPING MY KEY PEOPLE GET SOMETHING
THEY WOULD LIKE. I'LL DO THIS BY:

_____

_____

_____

_____

_____

_____

_____

_____

HERE'S WHY I'LL DO THIS:

_____

_____

_____

_____

_____

_____

_____

_____

Being Humble Is Not
Weakness or Meekness

One of the most fundamental lessons of leadership is that if you're a leader, it's not about you.
It is about the people following you. The best leaders devote almost all of their energy
to inspiring and developing others.

George Bradt, author, consultant, and *Forbes* contributor

Being humble is not thinking less of yourself—it is thinking of yourself less. What I have learned over the years is that my job as a leader is like being a shepherd. It is about leading the team members—it's about them. I don't have to shine. It's about the mission and the team. As leaders, we need to be more conductor, less soloist.

Here are some tips:

- Create a system where everything doesn't have to funnel through you or a single person. Work to have a process that will increase accountability and distribute responsibility.
- Beware of the "Platform Paradox." When you have a "platform," that is, a position and a title, it is easy to get wrapped up in it and look for applause. Your platform should always be about service.
- Encourage others on the team to push back. You don't need yes people. You do need diversity of careful thinking and opinion, which leads to healthy discourse.
- Humble leaders maintain an others-first mindset. It is always about them. How can you help them get better?
- Set your intention on being approachable and vulnerable and realize it is not about you. I learned, I'm never as good as I think I am. I had to get over myself. How about you?

*T*ODAY, I WILL PRACTICE HUMILITY AND SHARING RESPONSIBILITY BY:

_____

_____

_____

_____

_____

_____

_____

_____

I WILL DO THIS BECAUSE:

_____

_____

_____

_____

_____

_____

_____

_____

_____

_____

Your Most Valuable Medium of Exchange

As a leader moves up in an organization, up to 90 percent of their success lies in emotional intelligence.

Daniel Goleman, author, *Emotional Intelligence*

Over the years, I have learned—and I am still learning—that the leader's most valuable medium of exchange is not money, nor is it IQ, multiple degrees, the number of wearable techno gizmos, industry experience, good looks, charisma, ability to create strategies and a business plan, read a profit and loss statement, and so on.

As a leader, my most valuable medium of exchange is emotional capital, in other words, the ability to connect with others. According to Goleman, there are three "primary derailers" that prevent or break emotional connection: "difficulty handling change, not being able to work well in a team, and poor interpersonal relations."

Building high-performing, lasting, profitable relationships with employees and customers requires that we embrace and ultimately rely on emotion in our work, which at the end of the day is deeply human.

Author and poet David Whyte wrote:

> *Listen. In every office you hear the threads of love and joy,*
> *And fear and guilt, the cries for celebration and reassurance,*
> *And somehow you know that connecting those threads is what*
> *You are supposed to do, and business will take care of itself.*

*T*ODAY, I WILL PRACTICE CONNECTING THE THREADS BY:

_____

_____

_____

_____

_____

_____

_____

I WILL DO THIS BECAUSE:

_____

_____

_____

_____

_____

_____

_____

_____

_____

The Three P's
of Engagement

Good leaders make people feel that they're at the very heart of things, not at the periphery.
Everyone feels that he or she makes a difference to the success of the organization,
and when that happens, people feel centered and that gives their work meaning.

Warren G. Bennis, author and leadership expert

As a leader, you know having your people engaged is critical toward achieving your goals. And yet, for many leaders, people engagement is one of their biggest challenges. The fact is, leading effectively is almost impossible without employee engagement. You cannot lead a board, committee, an individual or a team if they are not engaged.

As you build engagement within your team or organization, remember to find the balance between the three P's—purpose, passion, and process.

Keep these aspects in mind:

- If you have a purpose and are passionate about what you do, but lack a process, you will waste people's time.
- If you are passionate and have a process, but you lack a sense of purpose, you will be like a flare that burns brightly for a short period of time and then flames out.
- If you have a sense of purpose and process, but you lack passion, you will have a difficult time leading.

$\mathcal{T}$ODAY, I WILL PERIODICALLY CHECK IN WITH MYSELF ON THE THREE P'S OF ENGAGEMENT: DO WE HAVE A *PURPOSE*? AND DOES EVERYONE KNOW WHAT IT IS? CAN I ARTICULATE IT WELL? CAN OTHERS?

_____

_____

_____

_____

HOW IS MY *PASSION* FOR OUR PURPOSE, FOR OUR WORK, FOR OUR TEAM? HOW IS THEIR PASSION FOR OUR PURPOSE, FOR THEIR WORK, FOR ONE ANOTHER? HOW SOLID ARE OUR *PROCESSES* TO ENABLE THE PASSION TO FLOW AND THE PURPOSE TO RESONATE AND BE ACHIEVED?

_____

_____

_____

_____

WHERE DO ANY OF THESE NEED SHORING UP OR MODIFYING? HOW WILL I GO ABOUT THAT?

_____

_____

I WILL DO THIS BECAUSE:

_____

_____

Seek First
to Understand

When you really listen to another person from their point of view,
and reflect back to them that understanding, it's like giving them emotional oxygen.

Stephen R. Covey, educator, author, and businessman

Perhaps in addition to intelligence quotients and emotional quotients, we should have a scale for QQ—our questions quotient.

Seeking first to understand is one of Stephen R. Covey's *7 Habits of Highly Effective People.* In other words, before jumping to solutions, we need to make sure we are focusing on the right issue. By mastering the art of effective questioning, we can become problem solvers, coaches, and leaders.

As a quick reminder, here are a few rules:

- Avoid questions that result in a yes or no response.
- Avoid questions with hidden solutions.
- Avoid multiple-choice questions.

Ask open-ended questions:

- What is your desired outcome?
- What you have you already tried?
- Why is this important to you?
- What would this mean to you?
- What are you willing to commit to?

As leaders, we are always tempted to tell, talk too much, preach, etc. We need to be reminded that our intention is to change behavior and increase performance. People rarely change their performance by hearing us tell them what to do.

*T*ODAY, I WILL STRIVE TO HAVE BETTER QUESTIONS, NOT BETTER ANSWERS.
I WILL DO THIS WITH ONE OR TWO PEOPLE, INCLUDING:

_____

_____

I WILL DO THIS BY:

_____

_____

_____

_____

_____

_____

_____

_____

_____

_____

I WILL DO THIS BECAUSE:

_____

_____

_____

_____

Develop Your Internal Elevator Speech

Clarity is power. The clearer you are about what you want, the greater your chances of achieving it.

Billy Cox, motivational speaker and sales trainer

There is no question that everyone in your company should know the importance of building deep, authentic customer connections. There's a delicate balance between messaging financials, metrics, dashboards, and the customer experience. If you're spending too much time on the business and not enough time on the experience, danger may loom.

My recommendation is to develop an "elevator speech" for everyone in the company to make sure they get it.

To develop the speech, ask yourself the following questions:

Where are we going?

Paint an inspiring vision that includes the ideal relationship with the customer. Write it from the customer's point of view. What do you do that matters to them?

Why are we going there?

It has to be more than just money. What is deeply meaningful for all stakeholders?

Who is going with us?

Identify the key players who will lead in the messaging. They will connect and build the long-term relationships.

How are we going to get there?

This is an opportunity to emphasize and reinforce key elements in the strategy. Get buy-in from your top players.

Here's what I know to be true: create value first, then the money follows.

TODAY, I WILL FOCUS ON CREATING (OR UPDATING) OUR INTERNAL ELEVATOR SPEECH. I WILL RUN THROUGH THE QUESTIONS MYSELF AND THEN POSE THE SAME QUESTIONS TO (TWO PEOPLE):

_____

_____

AND GET THEIR PERSPECTIVES:

_____

_____

_____

_____

_____

_____

_____

_____

_____

HERE'S WHY I WILL DO THIS:

_____

_____

_____

_____

Don't Play
Robin Hood

Leaders who gather followers add to what they can accomplish.
Leaders who develop leaders multiply their ability.

John C. Maxwell, leadership expert and author

We are all aware of the Robin Hood effect—taking from the rich and giving to the poor. But in business, let's be sure we are giving our best to the best.

Typically, in most businesses, 80 percent of the results are driven by 20 percent of the people or customers. We call them the Top 20 Club. You have to be careful not to spend too much of your time with the 80 percent of people who produce only 20 percent.

As leaders, we need to invest our time where we will receive the best return on our time. Invest your time by listening to your Top 20. How can you better serve them? What could you and/or the company do more of? Less of? What should you start doing?

I have found that fair doesn't mean equal. Companies grow when the key people in the company grow. So, when you give your best to your best, *that* is nothing to apologize for. Actually, if you don't give your best to your best, that is worth apologizing for.

Remember, your best customers and your best performers want and deserve to be listened to. Be on purpose to add value to them—that is fair.

TODAY, I WILL LOOK FOR THOSE AREAS WHERE I MAY HAVE BEEN PLAYING
ROBIN HOOD. WHAT ARE THE DYNAMICS THAT ARE CAUSING ME TO DO THIS?
AND WHAT DO I NEED TO DO TO SHIFT?

_____

_____

_____

_____

_____

_____

WHO ARE MY TOP 20? WHO ARE THE COMPANY'S TOP 20?
WHAT DO I/WE NEED TO DO TO NURTURE AND BETTER SERVE THEM?

_____

_____

_____

_____

_____

THIS IS WHY I NEED TO HASH THIS OUT:

_____

_____

_____

_____

The Key to Positive Reinforcement

Lasting progress can only happen once we give up the urge to repeatedly say "No" to mistakes in favor of looking to say "Yes" to their successful behaviors.

Grey Stafford, zoologist, educator, and animal trainer

What I know to be true is, if we want better performance from our people, we must deliver feedback on their performance quickly, honestly, and consistently.

The *good:* psychologists tell us behaviors that are reinforced are often repeated. For many animals—humans included—positive reinforcement is like oxygen. I actually had a business leader tell me, "Why should I reinforce a compliment to someone I am paying to get the job done?"

You gotta be kidding, I thought. But he was serious. He is "old school"—I'm the boss, do what I say, etc. He dismissed the advice of positive reinforcement as "too soft." He continued with the sentiment that only when his employees knock it out of the park does he compliment them.

What a missed opportunity. His head was in the sand. He was simply ignoring how human nature works.

If someone does something right, makes a good decision, or engages in useful action, the leader must reinforce it if he or she wants to see more of it. The key to positive reinforcement is to deliver it quickly—because delayed consequences lose their punch. The same holds true for poor performance.

$\mathcal{T}$ODAY, I WILL EXAMINE WHETHER AND HOW I REINFORCE GOOD BEHAVIOR AND PRODUCTIVE HABITS. AM I REINFORCING WHAT IS POSITIVE?

_____

_____

_____

_____

_____

_____

_____

IF SO, HOW, AND AM I DOING THIS QUICKLY, HONESTLY, AND CONSISTENTLY?
IF I AM NOT, WHAT DO I NEED TO DO TO SHIFT?

_____

_____

_____

_____

_____

HERE'S WHY THIS IS IMPORTANT AND WHAT IT WILL MEAN FOR OUR TEAM:

_____

_____

_____

_____

If the head man in a company is not working 12 hours a day, doing things, taking risks, but also standing with his people in the trenches at the most difficult of times, then the company loses something.

Rupert Murdoch, media tycoon

A reminder to all of us who lead others: our office may be our own trap. We may have a private office, perhaps the "corner office,"—a reward for hard work, dedication, and getting results. But the physical office itself can be a trap. That may be an exaggeration, but be aware: To really know what is going on with the people, we must invest the time to get out there and talk with them. I call this LBWA—Leadership by Walking Around.

Walking around and visiting them is one of the best ways to learn what people are thinking. I know this consumes time, but I can tell you by all accounts the investment of time has brought great results.

When I first started my "walk arounds," people would almost jump to attention. It seemed like a surprise attack. After one or two times, the shock disappeared.

My so-called agenda was about them, and I soon discovered they could feel it. Simple questions like: What are you working on? What are you frustrated about? What could we do to give you more support? What is most exciting for you now?

You get the idea—make it about them, stay curious and be genuinely interested in learning about them.

Don't misunderstand: There is no substitute for one-to-one coaching and mentoring. However, that is not possible for everyone. Obviously, the size of the company is a factor. We need to pick our best opportunities to connect. I encourage you to do more LBWA. You will receive valuable information.

TODAY, I WILL MAKE THE TIME TO WALK AROUND AMONG MY TEAM AND SEE HOW THEY ARE DOING. I WILL FIND OUT WHAT THEY ARE WORKING ON, WHAT THEY ARE STRUGGLING WITH, AND WHERE I OR OUR LEADERSHIP MAY BE ABLE TO HELP.

I WILL MAKE NOTES OF WHAT I LEARN:

_____

_____

_____

_____

_____

_____

_____

_____

_____

_____

_____

I WILL DO THIS BECAUSE:

_____

_____

_____

_____

_____

_____

Our People
Want to Feel This

[Attunement] lets the other person know that we really get them—that we're by their side. This is an invaluable experience to receive and to offer another person.

Diane Poole Heller, therapist, author, and Adult Attachment Theory expert

Deep down, humans want to feel connected and to be known. Relationship coach Kyle Benson refers to this as attunement—the desire and willingness for someone to travel into your inner world to explore who you are and who you are becoming. Two people in attunement find resonance for a sustained connection. This connection cultivates trust.

Over time, every team member has challenging seasons in their lives. How we respond as leaders is crucial. Ideally, we would like our team members to leave their issues at home. In most cases, they can't; their challenges affect behavior in their daily duties as well as the duties of others.

Remember—developing a strong connection is the currency for a strong relationship. Key elements for us as leaders are to really listen and listen with empathy. Another thing I have learned to be true is that sometimes all a person needs is someone who believes in them and their ability to overcome. Our tendency is often to be the fixer when the solution may be simply to listen, encourage, and empower.

TODAY, I WILL CONSIDER: IS THERE SOMEONE ON MY TEAM WHO NEEDS ME JUST TO LISTEN? I WILL SEEK OUT THAT PERSON, LISTEN TO THEM WITH EMPATHY AND ENCOURAGE THEM. I WILL DO THIS BY:

_____

_____

_____

_____

_____

_____

_____

_____

_____

_____

_____

_____

I WILL DO THIS BECAUSE:

_____

_____

_____

_____

_____

_____

Look Under
the Hood

Great things are done by a series of small things brought together.

Vincent van Gogh, Impressionist painter

We have dashboards. Our car's dashboard tells speed, fuel level, engine temperature, etc. Our organizational dashboard has key metrics. I call these metrics dashboard knowledge. There is no question of the importance for understanding dashboard metrics and the general direction of the company.

Yet, as I have learned, dashboard metrics are less helpful for identifying specific actions, improvements, and adjustments for the company to run more smoothly. If we want this type of information, *we have to look under the hood.*

Like your car, if the business is running hot, sputtering, having acceleration issues, you must get under the hood to see what is happening. To effectively get under the hood in our companies, we need to get up close with the team, especially the key players.

We can learn what is really happening by asking questions and following up. It could be systems, processes, customer care, or employee engagement.

TODAY, I WILL CONSIDER HOW WELL I HAVE BEEN PAYING ATTENTION TO
WHAT'S REALLY GOING ON. I WILL CONNECT WITH (THREE INDIVIDUALS):

_____

_____

_____

_____

_____

AND I WILL ENGAGE WITH THEM ABOUT:

_____

_____

_____

_____

BASED ON WHAT I FIND OUT, I WILL:

_____

_____

_____

_____

I WILL DO THIS BECAUSE:

_____

_____

_____

Praise or Pay:
Which Matters More?

The deepest principle of human nature is the craving to be appreciated.

William James, philosopher, historian, and psychologist

For many years, I thought that money was *the* big motivator. People leave for more money —they got a better offer. But that is not always the case. Research suggests fair and competitive pay are important. However, the real factors in keeping the good employees are challenge, growth opportunities, flexibility, meaningful work—and a leader who values them. Bingo!

Certainly, perks are valuable and help in the recruiting process. But the research has proven that good ones won't stay because of perks. They want the non-monetary benefits listed above. Obviously, not everyone is motivated in the same ways. We need to discover what works best individually. Here are two more quotations to ponder when thinking about how you might begin to court the non-monetary benefits: From writer Gladys Bronwyn Stern, "Silent gratitude isn't much use to anyone." Love that one! And, "Compensation is a right; recognition is a gift."

We can focus on the non-monetary by giving our people private and public praise and recognition; by being specific when we do so; and even by giving them hand-written notes (anyone can send a text or email).

$\mathcal{T}$ODAY, I WILL CONSIDER HOW I AM SHOWING MY APPRECIATION TO THOSE
ON MY TEAM. IS THERE ANYTHING I COULD DO BETTER IN THAT ARENA?

_____

_____

_____

_____

_____

_____

_____

_____

_____

I WILL DO THIS BECAUSE:

_____

_____

_____

_____

_____

They Follow Character

In matters of style, swim with the current; in matters of principle, stand like a rock.

Thomas Jefferson, 3rd U.S. President, Declaration of Independence principal author

Being an influential leader is as much about who you are as it is about what you do. Our character is rooted in our values. And our values—not our circumstances or our feelings—guide our decisions and behavior.

Because we are leaders, our people always observe what we model. Our challenge is to live our values. Of course, choosing values is a personal matter, but I'd like to examine three here:

INTEGRITY. There is no question about the importance of your personal integrity when it comes to coaching and inspiring others to action. Our integrity is challenged every day. Doing the *right thing* may not always be the most expedient thing, but know *you are never sorry when you do the right thing.*

HUMILITY. Again, this isn't thinking less of yourself; it is thinking of yourself less. Coaching and leading is always about the *other person.* True humility is expressed best in *our actions,* not our words.

CARING. The value of caring is expressed as a *genuine interest in others.* Our people want to know if we prioritize their interests above our own. That is always demonstrated in our actions, in our behavior.

Integrity, humility, and caring are the foundational values of inspiring leadership. Building a team is like building a house—it starts with a solid foundation.

TODAY, I WILL CONSIDER WHERE I STAND IN RELATION TO THOSE I LEAD WITH
RESPECT TO MY CORE VALUES, INCLUDING INTEGRITY, HUMILITY, AND CARING.
HOW AM I DOING WITH EACH OF THESE?

_____

_____

_____

_____

AMONG THESE AND MY OTHER CORE VALUES, WHERE CAN I IMPROVE WHAT I AM
MODELING OR HOW?

_____

_____

_____

_____

I'LL CHOOSE ONE OF THESE TO IMPROVE, AND HERE'S HOW I'LL DO THAT:

_____

_____

_____

_____

HERE'S WHY THIS IS IMPORTANT:

_____

_____

_____

What Are
You Reading?

Not all readers are leaders, but all leaders must be readers.

Harry Truman, 33rd U.S. President

Reading is an excellent way to tap into the experience of others—a great way to learn by connecting with others. It puts me in touch with someone I may never meet in person. It stimulates my mind. In turn, what I read can lead me to better actions, which then produce better habits, which lead to better results and a better life. Most of our reading should be centered around helping us to become better leaders.

How often has it happened that we're at work and looking up something in a book we've been reading when one of our staff or a stranger notices and says, "Oh, interesting! Tell me about that." That creates a perfect opportunity to share what we are learning which, in turn, may inspire that person.

As you progress on your leadership journey, you'll find books can be helpful with your consulting and coaching activities. Some of my favorite writers on these topics include John Maxwell, Dave Anderson, and Peter Lencioni. If you took at a peek inside my well-utilized business books, you would find notations, my own personal index in the back of pages or sections I have found to be important, as well as quotations I periodically ponder.

One book I have found especially helpful for all facets of leadership is *The 4 Disciplines of Execution* by Chris McChesney, Sean Covey, and Jim Huling. The authors provide a simple and repeatable proven formula for executing the most important priorities. Examples: Making sure everyone knows the score at all times, so your team will know whether they are up or down. The idea is "people play differently when they are keeping score."

That's just one of many examples of the books I have found most helpful in my own leadership journey.

TODAY, I WILL COMMIT TO SPENDING AT LEAST 10 MINUTES READING A BOOK ABOUT LEADERSHIP. I WILL SHARE SOMETHING I AM LEARNING FROM THAT BOOK WITH:

_____

AND I WILL ENCOURAGE THIS PERSON TO READ IT, TOO.

I WILL DO THIS BECAUSE:

_____

_____

_____

_____

_____

_____

_____

_____

_____

_____

_____

_____

_____

_____

The Buck
Stops Here

Employees want to feel good about their organization and what it offers the world.
They want to be able to say, "I like what this company stands for." If employees
do not believe in their company or do not believe the company can successfully uphold
its brand or reputation, they are likely to look for a different job.

Gallup State of the American Workplace (2017)

Depending on your age, you may not be aware of the slogan, "The buck stops here." U.S. President Harry Truman (1945-1953) had a sign on his desk in the Oval Office that said that. At the time, the phrase became very popular. Even though that was decades ago, it applies just as much today. As a leader, responsibility begins and ends with you.

Regardless of your capacity—CEO, district supervisor, department head, school principal, project manager—you count the most when it comes to retention.

People join people and people leave people. You can have the best-paying jobs in your industry and among your competitors, but if you do not do what's necessary to drive employee engagement, satisfaction and commitment—all of which are within your control—they will leave.

The questions are: How are you connecting with your best people? How often? Are you listening to them? Because, believe it, they want to be heard. The most important things in our organizations are not things; the equipment, the building, the office furniture. The most important things are people, in particular, our key winners. Why would we not invest our time in them? Coach them? Mentor them? We have the influence and power to make a difference.

*T*ODAY, I WILL CONSIDER WHETHER THERE IS SOMEONE WITH WHOM
I NEED TO CONNECT, AND I WILL FOLLOW THROUGH BY:

_____

_____

_____

_____

_____

_____

_____

_____

AND SEE WHAT HAPPENS.

THIS IS IMPORTANT TO ME BECAUSE:

_____

_____

_____

_____

_____

_____

_____

_____

The Je Ne Sais Quoi of Leadership

People who love life have charisma because they fill the room with positive energy.

John C. Maxwell, leadership expert and author

What is charisma? In Greek mythology, the Kharites were the Three Graces—personifying good cheer, beauty, and mirth and merriment—who attended the goddess of love, Aphrodite. In our world, good leaders have charisma, and it's easier to describe being on the receiving end than it is to outline the mechanics of its composition. Charisma feels like an attraction, and it's contagious. For me, it compels me to want to be around that person because, not only are they likable, but I know I can benefit from being around them because they make me better when I am.

The charismatic leader is knowledgeable and passionate about their work. They are confident in what they do and how they behave. That confidence inspires fascination and devotion. It's a mistake to think the charismatic leader has to be gregarious; a quiet leader can also demonstrate charisma, and charisma demonstrated is the kind that connects with focused attention on the other person, eye contact, listening, not talking, and expressing empathy. The charismatic leader helps the person talking feel important.

*T*ODAY, I WILL ASSESS MY CHARISMA AS A LEADER. WHEN DO I DEMONSTRATE IT THE MOST? THE LEAST?

_____

_____

_____

_____

_____

_____

_____

_____

AND WHAT CAN I DO TO MORE CONSISTENTLY SHOW IT?

_____

_____

_____

_____

I WILL DO THIS BECAUSE:

_____

_____

_____

_____

The Smart Six

The concept here is to have **smart goals in each area** of life.

SPIRITUAL
More time with God. Prayer, reading, and church attendance. Meet with a group.

PHYSICAL
Exercise. Better nutrition. Less sugar.

MENTAL
Take a course, a seminar. Read (fiction and non-fiction).

PERSONAL
Volunteering. More family time. Date night.

PROFESSIONAL
Improve a skill set. Acquire new knowledge. Seek a mentor.

FINANCIAL
Increase savings. Increase net worth. Acquire property.

A smart goal is specific, measurable, attainable, relevant, and time bound.
Identify two to three smart, 12-month goals in each category.

CHAPTER THREE

Mastering Communication

All leaders—whether they are at the peak of a Fortune 100 company, a five-person design shop, a lighting importer/distributor, or a medium-sized grocer—are in the communication business. And skilled communication is at the heart of adept leadership.

Communication that facilitates understanding garners trust and makes clear what is expected is critical to everyone's success and the success of a business or organization. Clear communication eliminates conflicts, dashed expectations, dis-ease, and eroding trust.

When it comes to making every day your masterpiece, communication skills are your most important tools. This section affords leaders the opportunity to explore and hone these skills. Skilled communication, like so many other leadership-critical qualities, starts within—in how we talk to ourselves. So, among the entries included here, you will find a mix that relates to inwardly directed as well as outwardly directed communication.

How Is Your Verbal Communication?

To effectively communicate, we must realize that we are all different in the way we perceive the world and use this understanding as a guide to our communication with others.

Tony Robbins, entrepreneur, author, and motivational speaker

We know how critical communication is, in particular verbal communication. Words are powerful and carry plenty of weight, and the weight is heavier when you are the leader. The weight is heavier when you are the leader. Effective communication involves not just talking, but also careful listening as well as expressing interest and empathy.

Here are some tips to improve your verbal communication:

- Make an effort to put yourself in the other person's role and anticipate how your communication is likely to be received.
- Always use open-ended questions to gather feedback and opinions.
- *Listen, listen, listen, and listen* some more.

Now evaluate yourself on a scale of 1 to 10 (10 being the highest) for each of the following:

- I am clear in my enunciation, grammar, and word choice.
- My tone, expression, and pace are in line with the intentions of my delivery.
- I am aware of my body language.
- I can convey my ideas in a concise and professional way.
- I regularly demonstrate empathy.
- I avoid excessive jargon.

TODAY, I WILL WORK ON ONE OF THE AREAS IN WHICH I DO NOT SCORE WELL.
I WILL PRACTICE WITHIN THIS AREA BY:

_____

_____

_____

_____

_____

_____

_____

_____

_____

_____

_____

AND I WILL DO THIS BECAUSE:

_____

_____

_____

_____

_____

Ask Questions

The wise man doesn't give the right answers; he poses the right questions.
Claude Lévi-Strauss, anthropologist and ethnologist

In developing people, we must cultivate the habit of curiosity. At times, this can be challenging; we are busy and want to get to the bottom of something. Nurturing curiosity requires creativity and intentionality—and this takes time.

Questions underpin curiosity. Asking questions keeps you informed, in touch, and aware. How many of us invest time in developing good questions prior to a one-on-one meeting?

Here is an idea to consider: Set aside 10 minutes before your one-on-ones and jot down critical questions. Make sure they are open-ended to inspire dialogue. During your meeting, *stay curious;* ask more questions as the conversation unfolds. Remember, leaders don't learn when they are talking; we learn when we listen intently.

See yourself as others' thinking partner. Your questions will bring out better thinking, which can lead to better behavior, which can lead to improved results. Isn't that the outcome we all want?

Today, I will consider how I present myself in relation to asking questions. Either with a set one-on-one meeting or less formally, I will take care in the questions I pose. I will do this by:

_____

_____

_____

_____

_____

_____

_____

_____

_____

_____

_____

_____

_____

_____

_____

_____

AND I WILL DO THIS BECAUSE:

_____

_____

_____

_____

_____

Leaders Cannot Overcommunicate

*Communication is to an organization like water is to a garden;
it keeps things vital, growing and healthy.*

John Hamm, author, *Unusually Excellent*

It's simple: When we take on the role of leader, we implicitly acknowledge we also act as the Chief Communication Officer—the CCO. Communication is at the core of leadership. If we follow John Hamm's analogy, then what leader does not want an organization that is vital, growing, and healthy? Hamm further points out, "Our people are like the plants—if they are neglected, they show signs of drought early and live in distress until we return them to a hydrated state."

This is an excellent illustration for us to ponder. When we are effectively communicating, we open doors for increased productivity and effectiveness. The bottom line is we cannot over-communicate. This is true especially when our organizations are undergoing significant change —a merger or an acquisition or departmental cuts.

Our people want and need to hear from us: "What is going on? Where do we stand? Where are we going? How do we get there?" And most important, "Where do I fit in the picture, and what does this mean for me?"

As you may well know, lack of communication can result in concern, worry, frustration, and even distraction. Not good outcomes.

Of course, we want to keep people informed. Often, the issue is neglect; we are "too busy"— a form of tyranny of the urgent, which we need to watch out for because it can be a killer. Simple awareness is the best solution. Keep them informed—keep communicating. You are the leader, and your opinions, thoughts, and ideas are important.

$\mathcal{T}$ODAY, I WILL CONSIDER THE PEOPLE ON MY TEAM AND ASK MYSELF WHERE I AM FALLING SHORT IN KEEPING THEM INFORMED, BECAUSE I AM "TOO BUSY" OR FOR OTHER REASONS. ONCE I KNOW THAT, HERE ARE THE STEPS I WILL TAKE TO REMEDY THIS (I'LL INCLUDE HERE WHAT I NEED TO MAKE THIS WORK):

_____

_____

_____

_____

_____

_____

_____

_____

_____

_____

_____

AND I WILL DO THIS BECAUSE:

_____

_____

_____

_____

The main thing is to keep the main thing the main thing.

Stephen R. Covey, educator, author, and businessman

Individuals and companies with too many priorities have no priorities at all. They risk spinning their wheels. Conversely, laser-focusing everyone on a single priority creates clarity and power throughout the organization. Both modes are easily felt within an organization or on a team. Scattered priorities lead to muddy communication—one person says one thing, one person hears something a certain way and, before you know it, people are working at cross purposes. Laser-focused priorities support clear communication and are akin to proper color mixing in painting—you get the colors you intended. Of course, this takes time.

As leaders, one of our responsibilities is to seek alignment from key team members on the priority. For example, you could ask, "If we could do only one thing this week, month, quarter, etc., what would that be?"

Get agreement, get commitment, and start the plan. We all spend plenty of time in strategy meetings. Let's be sure we walk out the door with *the main thing*.

Today, I WILL MAKE TIME TO ASSESS OUR TEAM'S PRIORITIES AND HOW WE
ARE COMMUNICATING THEM. WHERE ARE THINGS CLEAR? ARE THEY AS CLEAR AS
I THINK THEY ARE? IF NOT, HOW IS THIS SHOWING UP IN OUR WORK?
AND WHAT DO WE NEED TO DO TO GET CLEAR?

_____

_____

_____

_____

_____

_____

_____

_____

_____

_____

_____

_____

_____

I WILL ASSESS OUR PRIORITIES AND HOW WE COMMUNICATE THEM BECAUSE:

_____

_____

_____

_____

Stay Curious
and Seek Connection

Good leaders ask great questions that inspire others to dream more, think more, learn more, do more, and become more.

John C. Maxwell, leadership expert and author

What a lot of people miss is the power of asking questions and then being locked into the answer. For people to feel your connection, when they feel you are listening to them, not just hearing them—takes a lot of practice.

What is the first thing that comes to mind when you hear the word "conversation"? Typically, the answer is talking. But did you know that 80 percent of a successful conversation is listening?

Great conversationalists have one thing in common. They ask questions that draw out others. Why is that? It is a simple truth: people like to talk about their favorite subject, which is themselves.

To foster great conversation, I've come up with an easy technique called the 2C's: curiosity and connection.

- Be curious: Early in the conversation ask questions—what, how, where, and when?
- Connect: Connecting questions begin with a what or a how or a where and tend to have a personal attachment—something about the person's family or their thought process—that allows us to build a bridge.

Truth be told, if you were to enter every conversation with a few good questions, you would be viewed as an amazing conversationalist.

Harvard neuroscientists say that talking about our own beliefs and opinions, rather than those of other people, stimulates our mesolimbic dopamine system. This effect is most associated with the motivation and reward feelings we get from food, money, and sex. So, if you need proof for why becoming a curious and connecting conversationalist is important, the neuroscientists at Harvard just gave it to you.

TODAY, I WILL CONSIDER HOW I CAN BECOME MORE CURIOUS AND WORK TO CONNECT WITH OTHERS—ON MY TEAM, IN MY FAMILY, IN MY COMMUNITY.

I WILL CHOOSE ONE OR TWO OF THEM AND DO THIS BY:

_____

_____

_____

_____

_____

_____

_____

_____

_____

_____

_____

_____

_____

_____

I WILL DO THIS BECAUSE:

_____

_____

_____

_____

A Teachable Spirit

Be willing to be a beginner every single morning.

Meister Eckhart, theologian, philosopher, and mystic

Learning is a lifelong pursuit. To effectively lead—and influence—others, we must continually be learning and remain teachable. No matter how advanced we may be, we have so much to learn. The question every leader needs to ask is, "How teachable am I?"

We need to maintain "instinctive curiosity," because every situation, circumstance and engagement offers teaching moments—if we are present to notice. Being present means staying vigilant about and overcoming the major obstacle blocking our path: our pride. Guarding against and eliminating the "I'm superior" mindset keeps us humble and clear-eyed to see the learning opportunities in every situation.

Author, speaker, and pastor John Maxwell calls this a "teachable spirit" and developed 10 attributes of leaders with teachable spirits. Ask yourself:

1　Am I open to other people's ideas?
2　Do I listen more than I talk?
3　Am I open to changing my opinion based on new information?
4　Do I readily admit when I'm wrong?
5　Do I observe before acting on a situation?
6　Do I ask questions?
7　Am I willing to ask a question that will expose my ignorance?
8　Am I willing to ask for directions?
9　Am I open to doing things in a way I haven't done before?
10　Do I act defensively when criticized, or do I listen openly for the truth?

*T*ODAY, I WILL CONTEMPLATE THESE QUESTIONS AND EVALUATE MYSELF.
I WILL CHOOSE ONE THAT COULD USE MY ATTENTION AND WORK ON
IT THROUGHOUT THE DAY. I WILL DO THIS BY:

_____

_____

_____

_____

_____

_____

_____

_____

_____

_____

_____

_____

I WILL DO THIS BECAUSE:

_____

_____

_____

_____

Marking Change

I do not think much of a man who is not wiser today than he was yesterday.
Abraham Lincoln, 16th U.S. President

Because I am always challenging myself to learn, I ask myself both simple and profound questions. Two of the latter I ask myself once a year: "How have I changed from last year at this time?" And "How will I be different next year at this time?"

The next 12 months are filled with challenges and opportunities. As a lifelong learner, commitment to improving and growing is critical. Yet, improvement and growth are a matter of choice; personal and professional growth don't just happen. We must be intentional with daily habits that address the change required. Ultimately, we either maintain the status quo or grow. The choice is ours.

For example, when asking the question "How will I be different next year?" be specific: What new knowledge do I want to acquire? What new habits do I need to form, or which old ones to break? What new skills do I want to acquire?

Remember this: All progress starts with telling yourself the truth.

As leaders, our priority is to address reality. What is happening? What needs to change? When we get real, the next step is to put a plan in place with built-in accountability for execution. Our victory is won daily.

$\mathcal{T}$ODAY, I WILL PONDER THESE QUESTIONS AND ANSWER TRUTHFULLY:
HOW HAVE I CHANGED OVER THE PAST YEAR AND HOW WILL I BE DIFFERENT
THIS TIME NEXT YEAR?

_____

_____

_____

_____

_____

I WILL FOLLOW THROUGH WITH A PLAN THAT HAS BUILT-IN
ACCOUNTABILITY. IT MAY INCLUDE NEW HABITS TO FORM, NEW SKILLS
AND NEW KNOWLEDGE SUCH AS:

_____

_____

_____

_____

_____

_____

I WILL DO THIS BECAUSE:

_____

_____

_____

_____

Learning Leadership

In a static world, leaders can learn virtually everything that they need to know in life by the time we are fifteen, and few of us are called on to provide leadership.
In an ever-changing world, we can never learn it all. So, the development of leadership skills becomes relevant to an ever-increasing number of people.

John P. Kotter, author and Harvard Business School professor emeritus

In *Leadership Change,* John P. Kotter identifies four critical mental habits that support lifelong learning (and, no surprise, they involve communication):

- Risk-taking: Are you willing to leave your comfort zone? This is not "blind faith," but planning and preparation. Learning comes with risk; there is everything right with experimenting.

- Humble self-reflection: Are you being honest with what's going on? Whether your experience has been positive or negative, both provide learning opportunities, but only with honest reflection.

- Soliciting opinions: Are you open to others' thoughts, ideas, and information?
  Be aggressive about seeking the advice and opinions of others. Believe every encounter is a learning opportunity.

- Careful listening: As a lifelong learner, do you listen carefully? Develop a propensity to listen to others with humility and an open mind.

All of these are simple enough, right? What trips us up is our desire for immediate success. All of these are hard work, and it takes time and discipline for these to become habits. But, as leaders committed to lifelong learning, we stay focused on the big picture: The more we learn, the more value we can add to others in our lives who mean a great deal to us.

TODAY, I WILL ASK MYSELF THE FOUR QUESTIONS. I WILL CHOOSE THE ONE THAT COMES LEAST EASILY AND PRACTICE WORKING ON IT THROUGHOUT THE DAY BY:

_____

_____

_____

_____

_____

_____

_____

_____

_____

_____

_____

_____

I WILL DO THIS BECAUSE:

_____

_____

_____

_____

To Enforce
or Reinforce?

Leadership is the art of getting someone to do something you want done, because they want to do it.

Dwight D. Eisenhower, 34th U.S. President

To enforce or reinforce—that is the question. As leaders, we need to understand the difference. When leading people, we can use iron-fisted enforcement or positive recognition and reinforcement.

Let's check Webster on the definitions. Enforce—this implies controlling, forcing something to happen, making sure a rule or law is obeyed. Reinforce—this means making something stronger, supporting, helping, amplifying.

Both words denote getting results from an individual or team. However, the way these results are achieved is very different. I am certain your people don't wake up every morning and say, "I can't wait to go to work today and be controlled, manipulated, and managed." I am confident they are willing to be led by a leader who is interested in them and their growth.

I have learned effective leadership is about setting expectations and providing the right environment and resources for the team to achieve the expectations.

Being the reinforcer is not always about positive reinforcement. There are times where you must follow through on your stated consequences when performance is lacking.

The challenge here is how your team would describe you. Are you the enforcer or the reinforcer? How is your environment for growth? Do team members feel supported and strengthened?

TODAY, I WILL CONSIDER HOW I HAVE BEHAVED IN TERMS OF SEEKING TO
CONTROL THOSE ON MY TEAM VERSUS SEEKING TO SUPPORT THEM.
WHERE CAN I DO BETTER? HOW?

_____

_____

_____

_____

_____

_____

_____

_____

_____

_____

_____

I WILL DO THIS BECAUSE:

_____

_____

_____

_____

Teamwork Is Critical

Don't sit in your office and try to turn the numbers around. Get out in front and turn the people around, and they will turn the numbers around.

Dave Anderson, decorated combat veteran, author, radio host, and leadership consultant

The old acronym, TEAM (Together Everyone Achieves More) is so accurate. When everyone on the TEAM is collaborating, the magic happens.

One of the responsibilities of leaders is to attract, equip, and bring each member together. We do this by using the respective knowledge and skills of each member for the betterment of the cause; that's leadership.

Some key principles of teamwork and collaboration include the following:

MUTUAL RESPECT. As leaders, we must have the respect of those on the team, especially when it comes to collaboration. Team members need to have the confidence that if they share information, opinions, etc., they count and that they will be heard.

Mutual respect, by definition, is based on the belief that *everyone* has a valuable contribution to make. We must believe and communicate that everyone brings something to the table; each person has opinions, ideas and input. If we don't believe this, then what appears to be collaboration is nothing more than keeping people "in the loop."

INCLUSIVENESS. This principle is especially true with new initiatives. If it is your idea, bring together as many people as possible who will have a role in the project. This helps create "ownership" to them as individuals, not just you the leader. I have found when people feel like they have a sense of ownership, they feel empowered. When people are empowered as a team, the result of collaboration is victory.

Remember—working together precedes winning together.

TODAY, I WILL MAKE TIME TO CONSIDER HOW I FOSTER TEAM DYNAMICS. WHAT HAVE I DONE TO ENSURE THAT EACH PERSON HAS THE OPPORTUNITY TO CONTRIBUTE?

_____

_____

_____

_____

_____

_____

AM I BRINGING TOGETHER EVERYONE WHO HAS A STAKE IN A PROJECT? AND, IF I AM, AM I HELPING THEM TO FEEL EMPOWERED AROUND THEIR RESPONSIBILITY FOR THE PROJECT'S SUCCESS? IF I AM NOT DOING THESE THINGS, HOW CAN I SHIFT?

_____

_____

_____

_____

_____

I WILL DO THIS BECAUSE:

_____

_____

_____

Declare an End
to Poor Performance

Leaders set high standards. Refuse to tolerate mediocrity or poor performance.
Brian Tracy, author, speaker, and business/development consultant

As leaders, we create an environment where people come to work every day to prove themselves repeatedly. No one gets paid to budget their efforts or pace themselves. This is easier said than done, as I know rather painfully from experience. Too many compromises, too many hangers-on, too few performers.

Through the years, I have learned some actions that may help in putting an end to poor performance:

- Evaluate your roster and ask yourself whether you would re-hire your people. If not, it's time to exercise what is referred to as the 3 T's to turn things around: train, transfer, or terminate.
- Identify which poor performers are diminishing your standards.
- Be aware that keeping the wrong people affects the good ones, who are having water-cooler discussions on why you are keeping poor performers.
- Care enough to confront the poor performers when they are off-track. Delays may come back to bite you. I have been there.
- Also, be aware of the good performers who seem to be violating core values. They must be confronted, and you must have a zero-tolerance policy.

Remember—you will lose the respect of the best when you don't deal effectively with the worst.

$\mathcal{T}$ODAY, I WILL CONTEMPLATE WHAT I AM DOING TO SHRED POOR PERFORMANCE. IF I'M NOT DOING WHAT I NEED TO DO TO ELIMINATE IT, WHERE DO I NEED TO FOCUS MY ENERGY?

_____

_____

_____

_____

_____

_____

AM I TOLERATING THINGS I SHOULD NOT? IF SO, WHAT DO I NEED TO DO TO ALTER MY BEHAVIOR AND SET A NEW COURSE?

_____

_____

_____

_____

_____

I WILL CONTEMPLATE THIS AND TAKE ACTION BECAUSE:

_____

_____

_____

_____

Beyond the Words

The most important thing in communication is hearing what isn't said.

Peter Drucker, management consultant, educator, and author

One of the strongest human needs is to be heard. We all need people to listen to what we say as we have a need to be and feel valued.

Sometimes, we need to listen to more than just the words. People don't always say with words what they're really attempting to say. Their actual words and what they're trying to communicate are not always synonymous.

Dr. Albert Mehrabian, professor emeritus, University of California Los Angeles, has said communication effectiveness depends:

° 7 percent on the words we say

° 38 percent on the tone of voice

° 55 percent on non-verbal communication

Although Mehrabian's study was years ago, it is still relevant today. The point is, when we listen to people, let's pay attention to the tone of voice, gestures, body language, and their feelings and emotions.

$\mathcal{T}$ODAY, I WILL PAY CAREFUL ATTENTION TO THE CHARACTERISTICS OF COMMUNICATION EFFECTIVENESS IN MYSELF AND OTHERS. I WILL CONSIDER HOW THE NON-VERBAL COMMUNICATION MANIFESTS AND WHAT IT IS "SAYING." I WILL SEEK CLARITY AS NEEDED BY:

_____

_____

_____

_____

_____

_____

_____

_____

_____

_____

_____

_____

_____

_____

_____

I WILL DO THIS BECAUSE:

_____

_____

_____

_____

Clarity and Purpose

The most common sources of mistakes in management is the emphasis on finding the right answer rather than the right question.

Peter Drucker, management consultant, educator, and author

Many years ago while driving down the highway, it suddenly started to rain, and then it started to pour. This was bad enough, but my driver's side wiper was stuck. White-knuckled terror shot through me as I struggled to see the road ahead. The obvious choice of pulling over and waiting didn't seem promising in the event that a car behind me lost sight and drifted, so I decided to keep going at a snail's pace. The windshield caused anxiety, and I was filled with uncertainty on when I would reach my destination.

The same situation can happen with your team if they are unclear about where they are going and why. We all want to know that what we do makes an impact. I have learned that people are motivated to a higher performance when they understand how their efforts will contribute to the overall outcome. A *Harvard Business Review* study found that more than 60 percent of employees felt disconnected from their organization's purpose.

It is critical that our organizations and teams have a clearly articulated purpose statement that answers the following questions:

○ Why do we exist?

○ What value do we provide to our customers?

○ How are we uniquely positioned to deliver our value promise?

With many businesses in flux and dramatically changing their business model, now may be a good time to evaluate your purpose and mission statements. Do they answer the above questions? Enlist your team to ensure they are engaged and aligned with your organization's purpose and mission statements.

These actions go a long way toward keeping our metaphorical windshield wipers in shape and our vision clear.

*T*ODAY, I WILL MAKE THE TIME TO DO A CHECK-IN AROUND OUR ORGANIZATION'S AND MY TEAM'S PURPOSE STATEMENT AND TO LOOK AT HOW—AND HOW WELL —THIS HAS BEEN COMMUNICATED TO TEAM MEMBERS. CAN MY TEAM ANSWER THE QUESTIONS THAT INVOLVE OUR PURPOSE? IF NOT, HOW CAN I FACILITATE THEIR KNOWLEDGE AND HELP THEM TO UNDERSTAND THEIR VALUE TO OUR TEAM?

_____

_____

_____

_____

_____

_____

_____

_____

_____

_____

_____

_____

I WILL DO THIS BECAUSE:

_____

_____

_____

_____

Difficult
Team Members

If you have some respect for people as they are, you can be more effective in helping them to become better than they are.

John W. Gardner, World War II veteran, author, and former U.S. Health secretary

No one likes the idea of dealing with difficult people. Yet, as leaders, we have no choice; difficult people come with the territory.

In all my years, I believe I have experienced most of the types—arrogant know-it-alls, perpetual whiners, and Mr. & Ms. Excuses.

The truth is, we can't ignore these people. When these types of individuals aren't managed, they can become a plague in our organizations. Sometimes just one difficult person can wipe out an entire team's effectiveness.

What could be worse than not immediately dealing with these people? Your stronger team members experience your lack of addressing the issue and lose respect for your leadership abilities. If this practice continues, the best team members may leave. Remember, the stronger ones have options; the weaker ones don't and stay. Not a healthy situation.

I suggest trying the following when it comes to addressing difficult people effectively:

- Acknowledge the issue. When you learn of unacceptable behavior, don't ignore it. Gather facts and have the conversation with the person ASAP. In your conversation, it is critical you be level-headed and non-accusatory, and that you include a representation of factual examples.

- Target the behavior, not the person. The most effective way to address hard-to-deal-with people is to discuss the behaviors they've been displaying or actions they've been taking that are inappropriate or unacceptable. Stay with the facts. After you share your comments, stop talking and listen. Regardless of why they are doing what they are doing, we are never attacking them personally, just the behavior or actions.

- Get to the root of the problem and create a solution. Simply pointing out the behavior is not enough to create the change needed. Idle threats or demands to do better may not get the results. Being difficult is a learned behavior that oftentimes stems from fear and/or stress. Here is where good questioning demonstrates care and candor and must take place to get to the root cause. It's a good idea to ask the employee his or her ideas and thoughts on how the behavior or actions could change. You may be surprised.

The next step is to improve—or move on.

$\mathcal{T}$ODAY, I WILL ASSESS HOW I'VE BEEN HANDLING DIFFICULT PEOPLE. HAVE I BEEN LETTING BAD BEHAVIOR LINGER TOO LONG AND ALLOWING IT TO POISON THE GOOD WORK OF OTHERS? IF SO, HOW DO I NEED TO SHIFT THE DYNAMIC?

_____

_____

_____

_____

_____

WHAT KINDS OF EXAMPLES HAVE I GATHERED TO ILLUSTRATE THE BEHAVIOR? AND WHAT KIND OF CONVERSATION CAN I ENVISION HAVING WITH THE PERSON OR PEOPLE IN QUESTION?

_____

_____

_____

_____

_____

_____

I WILL UNDERTAKE THIS ASSESSMENT AND ACT ON WHAT I FIND BECAUSE:

_____

_____

_____

_____

Delegate!

If you want to do a few small things right, do them yourself.
If you want to do great things and make a big impact, learn to delegate.

John C. Maxwell, author, speaker, and pastor

One of the more challenging aspects of leading a growing organization is letting go and trusting others. As the organization begins to scale up to 50 or more employees, senior leadership must develop additional leaders who share the same values, passion, and knowledge of the business in order to effect change throughout the organization.

However, many leaders confuse delegation with abdication. Abdication is simply handing over a task to someone with no formal feedback mechanism. We need to be careful here. All systems need a feedback loop or they will eventually drift out of control. I have seen this happen; it can be costly and painful.

Successful delegation has four components:

PRIORITIES. Pinpoint what the person or team needs to accomplish. A great resource for this is the One Page Business Plan.®

MEASUREMENT. Create a system for monitoring progress. Consider developing key performance indicators (KPIs).

FEEDBACK. Provide feedback to the person and/or team. Set a meeting rhythm—regularly scheduled meetings with a defined purpose—to ensure everyone is on target and on course.

RECOGNITION. People want to feel valued and recognized. Never underestimate a simple "thank you" or my favorite, a handwritten note.

Today, I WILL ASSESS HOW I AM DOING WITH DELEGATING. AM I DELEGATING, AND, IF SO, HOW'S IT WORKING? ARE THE PRIORITIES RIGHT AND CLEARLY UNDERSTOOD?

_____

_____

_____

_____

DO I HAVE A WAY OF MARKING PROGRESS AS WELL AS ENSURING THAT PEOPLE KNOW THE PROGRESS—OR LACK—SO THEY CAN KEEP TO THE PRIORITIES?

_____

_____

_____

_____

AM I MAKING THE TIME TO SHOW THAT I VALUE THEM? IF I AM NOT DOING THESE THINGS, WHAT DO I NEED TO DO TO START? WHAT PROCESSES DO I NEED TO PUT IN PLACE?

_____

_____

_____

_____

I WILL ASSESS AND FOLLOW THROUGH BECAUSE:

_____

_____

How Is
Your Transparency?

[Leaders] are more interested in understanding reality than in being right and are not afraid to accept that they were wrong. This allows them to welcome criticism—not because they like it any more than the rest of us, but because they know it's necessary in order to make progress.

Amy C. Edmondson, author and Harvard Business School professor

Tomas Chamorro-Premuzic, author, professor, and CIO, ManpowerGroup

Never let them see you sweat. Make sure you have all the answers (after all, you're the boss). Tell them what they need to know—nothing more; they can't handle it. Never admit mistakes; deflect if you can.

Sound familiar? This was the management style I was taught and the mindset I thought leaders possessed. Thankfully, it didn't take long to realize that people want—and deserve—authentic leadership. You want authentic people on your team, so make sure you're leading with integrity, which includes transparent communication.

Here are four simple ways you can boost your level of transparency and authenticity, and likely increase trust, productivity, and respect among those in your organization and on your team:

- Let others know who you are and what makes you tick (the good, the bad, and the ugly). It's OK to admit and show weaknesses. They already know them anyway. When you openly admit your mistakes, your leadership stock goes up, and you remind your team that you're human.

- Communicate openly and candidly. Share the dirty details about upcoming decisions. The proverbial water cooler dries out quickly when important information isn't shared or not all the facts are given. Then you find yourself in damage-control mode.

- Disclose how and why you make key business decisions. Offering insight into how you make decisions enables the team both to understand your thinking process and learn from it.

- Be consistent. You want to be predictable. When your team wonders which side of the fence you are on today, they also wonder how much they can trust and respect you and your abilities as their leader.

Today, I will assess how transparent I am with my team. Do they know me and how I make decisions? Am I consistent in my communications? Do I make a point to share important information with them?

_____

_____

_____

_____

_____

_____

_____

_____

_____

_____

If I am falling short in any of these areas, what do I need to do to shift and how will that look and feel?

_____

_____

I will look at how transparently and authentically I communicate because:

_____

_____

_____

How Is
Your Listening?

No man would listen to you talk if he didn't know it was his turn next.

Edgar Watson Howe, novelist, and newspaper and magazine writer and editor

I love this quote. It's comical, but it has the ring of truth.

Most leaders like to talk. We know communication is an essential leadership tool, but do we place the same level of emphasis and importance on active listening as we do on communicating? We should.

Unfortunately, Howe's aphorism may describe the way too many of us approach communication: People are too busy waiting for their turn to talk to really focus on the conversation and gain knowledge and insight into what the other person is sharing. Are you guilty of that? I know I have been.

When U.S President Lyndon B. Johnson was a senator from Texas, he kept a sign on his office wall that read, "You ain't learnin' nothin' when you're doin' all the talkin.'"

Our ability to skillfully listen is one of the key ways to gain influence with others. And, of course, leadership is about influence.

Consider the following benefits of truly listening:

- Listening shows respect.
- Listening builds relationships.
- Listening increases knowledge.
- Listening generates ideas.
- Listening builds loyalty.

One of the foremost human needs is to be understood. If you are married, you know what I mean—just ask your spouse. It is through listening that we come to understand others, and to paraphrase U.S. President Woodrow Wilson, our leader ears should be ringing with the voices of the people in our organizations and on our teams.

TODAY, I WILL REFLECT ON HOW WELL I HAVE BEEN LISTENING. WHEN SOMEONE TALKS, AM I THINKING ABOUT WHAT I WANT TO SAY—OR AM I HOLDING THE MENTAL SPACE OF ATTENTION FOR WHAT THEY ARE EXPRESSING?

_____

_____

_____

_____

_____

_____

IF I AM NOT DOING THIS, WHAT DO I NEED TO DO TO SHIFT? IF I HAVE BEEN DOING THIS, WHAT ARE SOME OF THE THINGS I FEEL GRATEFUL FOR LEARNING?

_____

_____

_____

_____

_____

I WILL DO THIS BECAUSE:

_____

_____

_____

_____

Delegate? Yes.
But to Whom?

The best executive is one who has sense enough to pick good people to do what he wants done, and self-restraint enough to keep from meddling with them while they do it.

Theodore Roosevelt, 26th U.S. President

In every organization, the leader is faced with the challenge of delegating. It could be a task, managing a project, executing a large initiative, but it's not always the leader who is involved. In fact, in many cases, the leader most likely is not the best person for the job.

When considering whether a team member is the right fit for a possible task, here are a few things to ask:

- ◦ Do they have the time?
- ◦ Is this something they've expressed interest in?
- ◦ Do they have the skills needed to complete the task effectively? How much coaching, if any, is required?
- ◦ Do they typically meet deadlines?
- ◦ Will they work well with others?

It is critical that you clarify expectations and communicate the why behind your delegation. Otherwise, you risk dumping, not delegating.

Consider the following framework:

State the *why*. Clarify why the task, project, initiative, etc., is important.

State the *what*. Articulate what success looks like and how it will be measured.

Discuss the *how*. Describe the guidelines, resources, accountability, and impact of the specific task.

Lastly, always celebrate the victories. Nothing is more powerful than an empowered team that is all in.

TODAY, I WILL TAKE STOCK OF ANY TASKS, PROJECTS, OR INITIATIVES THAT NEED NOT ME, BUT OTHERS. I WILL CONSIDER WHO IS THE RIGHT PERSON FOR THE JOB, AND I WILL DEVELOP THE RATIONALE—THE WHY, WHAT, AND HOW—BEHIND CHOOSING A PARTICULAR TEAM MEMBER BEFORE I PROCEED.

_____

_____

_____

_____

_____

_____

_____

_____

_____

_____

_____

_____

I WILL DO THIS BECAUSE:

_____

_____

_____

_____

The Five Components
of Speaking

It's often very expensive to think out loud.

Minna Thomas Antrim, writer

We have many opportunities to speak to groups, teams, classrooms of students, etc. These are times to share knowledge, vision, mission, new initiatives or projects, and much more.

Here are five components of effective communication and speaking:

The art of the start. Capture attention with a strong opening statement. Communicate the *why*—what is in it for the audience?

Keep it relevant. The message should be rooted in the future and aligned with positive change. The past can be helpful for context. Use simple terms.

Have a key theme. Make your message "sticky," because when it is relevant and profound, you hold their attention.

Use pictures/stories. Everyone loves a good story, and a story or picture can help to drive your theme.

Call to action. Communicate the desired outcome. What does success look like? Always challenge them with action steps.

These communication techniques can be effective even when not speaking to a group.

TODAY, I WILL ASSESS HOW I AM DOING IN EACH OF THESE AREAS WHEN I AM WORKING WITH MY TEAM. DO I OPEN WITH SOMETHING RIVETING OR WITH A SNOOZE? DO I STAY ON POINT, AND IS WHAT I AM SAYING RELEVANT TO THE WORK OF THE TEAM?

_____

_____

_____

_____

HOW WELL AM I USING STORIES TO ILLUSTRATE MY POINTS? DO I LEAVE OFF BY GIVING THEM A SENSE OF WHAT SUCCESS WILL LOOK AND FEEL LIKE?

_____

_____

_____

_____

IF I AM TEPID IN ANY OF THESE AREAS, WHERE AND HOW CAN I HEAT THINGS UP?

_____

_____

_____

_____

I WILL DO THIS BECAUSE:

_____

_____

_____

How Is
Your Alignment?

There is an old Native American proverb: Tell me, and I'll forget.
Show me, and I may not remember. Involve me, and I'll understand.

Tom Nelson, pastor and president, Made to Flourish

By alignment, I'm not referring to your golf swing or the tires on your car. I am talking about your people and their alignment with your goals, vision, and mission. We can't simply hope for alignment; we need assurance we have it.

When it comes to determining if your team is in alignment, take the following actions in these three critical areas:

Always share what is going on. The good ones want to know! Help them understand the *why*. The why engages them.

Always ask for input. Demonstrate your excellent listening skills by just listening. Let them know you heard them.

Always seek commitment. You have a better opportunity to gain a commitment when the team is involved.

We need to remember that through emotional connection we can have the greatest alignment. When they know the *why* and are involved, then you have the head and the heart—it's called emotional connection, which facilitates alignment.

Today, I WILL CONSIDER HOW WELL I AM FACILITATING ALIGNMENT AMONG MY TEAM MEMBERS. HOW AM I SHARING? HOW AM I LISTENING? AM I SEEKING THEIR INVOLVEMENT CONSISTENTLY?

_____

_____

_____

_____

_____

_____

IF I AM NOT DOING WELL IN THESE AREAS, THEN WHAT DO I NEED TO DO TO SHIFT? IF I AM, THEN WHAT ARE THE FRUITS WE ARE ENJOYING?

_____

_____

_____

_____

_____

I WILL CONSIDER HOW WELL I AM DOING WITH ALIGNMENT BECAUSE:

_____

_____

_____

_____

Establishing Trust?

*The ability to establish, grow, extend, and restore trust is
the key professional and personal competency of our time.*

Stephen M. R. Covey, speaker, author, and business consultant

Every leader wants an environment where all team members feel they play an integral role and that they are contributing to the good of the organization. When this happens, we get results. To build an environment like this, we must start with trust. This is not new. We know this. The question is, establishing and maintaining *trust* may seem natural and easy, but how do we do it?

I have found we must demonstrate and show people we *believe* and *care* about them. Here are four steps you can take that may help in establishing the needed *trust*.

Believe that your people want to contribute.

Here is what I know to be true: Most, if not all—maybe 99 percent—of people come to work wanting to do well and try hard. So, it is our duty to show up thinking about them the same way. Remember, you are the leader; it starts with you. If you don't trust people, why should they trust you?

Demonstrate that everyone counts.

Studies have that shown most successful companies have a culture where every person *feels valued.* No matter what their position, they know they matter, and their contribution makes a difference. Legendary UCLA basketball coach John Wooden used to liken his team to a car. One star player may be like a powerful engine, while others may be like nuts that hold the wheel, but if we lose the wheel, how good is the engine?

The more they know, the more they care.

Share information, provide data. Remember, you cannot overcommunicate. Take care that you do not under-communicate, because that will bite you—and it hurts.

Ask questions that promote insight.

Stay curious and spend some time with as many different employees as possible. What is in their head? How can you make their job better for them? Not a bad idea to seek the same of your customers. We are demonstrating care when we ask questions and really listen. Remember— trust is the currency of all relationships.

TODAY, I WILL CONSIDER HOW WELL I HAVE ESTABLISHED AND MAINTAINED
THE TRUST OF THOSE I LEAD. I WILL THINK ABOUT TRUST IN THE CONTEXT OF
HOW WELL I COMMUNICATE, WHETHER AND HOW WELL I TRUST OTHERS,
AND HOW WELL I AM INVESTING TIME IN THE MEMBERS OF MY TEAM.

_____

_____

_____

_____

_____

_____

_____

_____

_____

_____

_____

_____

I WILL DO THIS BECAUSE:

_____

_____

_____

_____

Unclear Expectations, Unclear Destinations

More information is always better than less. When people know the reason things are happening, even if it's bad news, they can adjust their expectations and react accordingly. Keeping people in the dark only serves to stir negative emotions.

Simon Sinek, author and leadership/motivational speaker

At its most basic level, the job of a coach is to equip team members with knowledge and tools to be successful. Leaders only succeed when their teams succeed.

In sports, winning the game begins before the game, with preparation and good practice. Preparation and practice do not guarantee a win, but lack of them almost certainly assures a loss.

In business, preparation and practice involve clear expectations. If there are expectation gaps, there will be execution gaps. In my experience, performance issues usually stem from not communicating clear expectations up front. Gaining alignment through clear expectations is the number-one job for the leader/coach. When we are clear with expectations, we and the team are easily aligned.

We need to be as specific as we can when setting expectations and not to assume too much. In this case, repetition is a good thing. And we should be able to answer the question, "How will I know if I have met the expectations?"

Our team requires answers to four fundamental questions:
- Where are we going? (These are our goals.)
- What are we doing to get there? (These are our plans.)
- How can I contribute? (These are our roles.)
- What's in it for me? (These are our rewards.)

*T*ODAY, I WILL CONSIDER HOW WELL I HAVE COMMUNICATED MY AND THE
ORGANIZATION'S EXPECTATIONS TO MY TEAM. DO THEY UNDERSTAND
HOW THEY'LL KNOW THEY HAVE MET THEM? HOW WELL ALIGNED ARE WE?

_____

_____

_____

_____

_____

_____

_____

_____

_____

_____

_____

_____

I WILL ASSESS THIS BECAUSE:

_____

_____

_____

_____

Three Words =
Deeper Commitment

I've learned that people will forget what you said, people will forget what you did, but they will never forget how you made them feel.

Maya Angelou, poet, memoirist, and civil rights activist

How would you like to start a positive ripple effect that will lead others to a deeper commitment? Three words may be just the right prescription. That's because positive, encouraging words plant the seeds of commitment. Once spoken, they grow into results.

We only have to say three simple words. Try a few of these out on your team or someone in your life you care about:

- I appreciate you.
- I trust you.
- You will succeed.
- I am sorry. (Make sure you mean it.)
- I can help.
- I understand you.
- I promise you. (Make sure you keep it.)
- I believe you.
- You inspire me.

I bet you could think of more. We need to remember that the results of our interactions are either positive or negative. Our words, coupled with our deeds, can change how people feel.

TODAY, I WILL CONSIDER HOW I CAN SHIFT MY COMMUNICATION IN SIMPLE
WAYS TO CREATE POSITIVE CHANGE WITHIN MY TEAM. HERE ARE SOME WAYS
I CAN DO THIS:

_____

_____

_____

_____

_____

_____

_____

_____

_____

_____

I WILL DO THIS BECAUSE:

_____

_____

_____

_____

When communication is unclear—when the message and delivery are inconsistent—we pay more attention to nonverbal cues to interpret meaning.

Albert Mehrabian, UCLA communications professor emeritus

Who hasn't experienced this: A customer service rep answers your call with an annoyed tone and says they will help solve your problem? How do you feel—are you confident they will resolve the issue? Or this: An audience member compliments you with an awkward smile and little enthusiasm. Do you believe you delivered an effective presentation?

Now put yourself in the place of the customer service rep and the audience member. Can you see what happened there?

When you synchronize your message and your delivery, others will perceive you as trustworthy, credible, sincere, and authentic. Matching your words and behavior—how you look and how you sound—makes your communication a complete package.

What your listeners hear, see, and feel is in harmony. Consistency of message and delivery builds trust, which in turn builds influence.

Bottom line: We want our message and delivery to be in sync. When it comes to message versus delivery, delivery wins every time. This is something to think about the next time you are presenting to a group or speaking with just one person. If message and delivery are not in sync, nonverbals will drive your message.

TODAY, I WILL CONSIDER NOT JUST THE "WHAT" OF MY COMMUNICATION, BUT THE "HOW." AM I OBSCURING MY MESSAGE WITH INCONSISTENT DELIVERY?

_____

_____

_____

_____

_____

_____

_____

IF SO, WHAT CAN I DO TO SHIFT?

_____

_____

_____

_____

I WILL DO THIS BECAUSE:

_____

_____

_____

_____

The How-to of Influence

Communication is the real work of leadership.

Nitin Nohria, professor, Harvard Business School

Many people think influence comes from power, authority, experience and position. These factors may affect your influence, but I have found they are not the most relevant.

Influence is all about communication. Communication is the foundation of influence. However, when discussing communication, influence rarely comes up.

The impact of communication on influence becomes even more significant when one considers we can never *not* communicate. Virtually everything we do professionally and personally communicates a message and therefore impacts—positively or negatively—our ability to influence others.

Authors Louis E. Boone and David L. Kurtz in *Contemporary Business* estimate that leaders spend about 80 percent of their time—6 hours and 24 minutes of every eight-hour day—in direct communication with others, whether on the phone, in meetings, via email, or in one-on-one conversations.

By the way, technology and social media don't help the cause with BTW, THX, LOL, and emoticons. Yes, there is a time and place for those, but they are not part of *influential* communication. Instead, influential communication comes down to how people experience you and their perceptions of you. This means the error-free words you speak convey your knowledge and credibility. Your posture and voice reveal your confidence. Your eye contact imparts your trustworthiness. And all of these are ways you demonstrate your genuine concern and care for others.

$\mathcal{T}$ODAY, I WILL CONTEMPLATE HOW MUCH TIME I SPEND IN
DIRECT COMMUNICATION WITH OTHERS AND HOW MUCH OF THIS
IS INFLUENTIAL COMMUNICATION.

_____

_____

_____

_____

_____

_____

I WILL ASSESS HOW WELL I AM HANDLING COMMUNICATION THAT IS INFLUENTIAL
—WHETHER WITH THE PEOPLE ON MY TEAM OR OTHERS IN WHOM I INVEST
MY TIME, AND I WILL ASK MYSELF HOW THEY ARE EXPERIENCING ME. IF NEEDED,
I WILL SEEK FEEDBACK, I WILL PRACTICE AND BE ACCOUNTABLE.

_____

_____

_____

_____

_____

_____

I WILL DO THIS BECAUSE:

_____

_____

_____

Today I Will

Today is all we have. Yesterday ended at midnight.
Tomorrow has no guarantees.

Today I will make better decisions.

Today I will be kinder.

Today I will add value to another.

Today I will express gratitude.

Today I will learn.

Today I will be more aware.

Today I will ask more questions.

Today I will love.

Today I will express humility.

Today I will be selfless.

Today I will give more.

Today I will practice discipline.

Today I will invest, not spend, my time.

Today I will bring more clarity.

Today I will reflect.

Today I will think of possibilities.

Today I will create.

Today I will be more focused.

Today I will eat healthier.

Today I will think more.

CHAPTER FOUR

Enhancing Coaching

In what I like to call the three C's of leadership—connecting, communicating, and coaching —coaching is akin to the revisions that go into a piece of music or writing, the re-dos that can make or break a work of art.

Where we test our mettle is as coaching leaders. But unlike with works of art, which by necessity have a limited frame, human development may know plateaus, but it knows no limits, for there is no end to how much someone can expand.

Likewise, there is no end of influence for leaders who take on the joyful challenges of coaching with an enthusiasm for the work of helping people grow.

The definition of coaching I like most says that coaching is the combined acts of listening, observing, analyzing performance, and delivering fast feedback. That last one is critical to keep from relegating our people to the no-grow gray zone, where they will be if we give squishy feedback rather than honest, consistent, and fast feedback. And if our people do not grow, our businesses do not grow. So, it is critical that we be in the trenches with our people, and not be, as author and leadership consultant Dave Anderson says, "remote-control leaders" who are more concerned about things than people.

By continually honing our skills of listening, observing, analyzing, and providing quick feedback, we become coaches, and that means our work is never a "one and done," but rather, ongoing and, done well, a fully engaging process.

As corporate trainer and author Brian Souza notes, "Coaching is not merely something that you, as a manager, must do. A coach is someone that you, as a leader, must become."

This may sound easy. For me, it was not. I had much to learn when I began coaching our leadership team, associates and advisors, and it was on-the-job training coupled with outside mentorship and education from authors I had never met, or in person from fellow leaders. This section offers many opportunities to grow yourself as a coach.

If the term "coach" puts you off, perhaps you can more readily consider yourself your team members' "learning partner" or "thinking partner," which is a phrase I really like. Becoming a thinking partner frees you from being the person with all the credentials and all the answers to become the person who helps the team members to think for themselves. Then, you're not inclined, as I like to say, to pick up other people's monkeys. I have picked up enough monkeys to populate a small jungle, and I know that doing so is unwise: Not only am I unable to grow in my own work, but I also forestall the growth of the members of my team. Yet, being the "answer person" had been my security blanket, because, after all, if I were not the one providing answers, then how useful or needed was I?

The fact is, we do not need followers; we need to grow more leaders and we do this through partnering with them—through asking questions, through body language, through fostering empathy within ourselves and sharing that with them. This can lead us to what therapist Diane Poole Heller calls "contingency," the sense that someone feels of "getting got" and "feeling felt." If I really understand you, there is power in that relationship, power in that connection. That kind of power is what changes people, changes organizations, changes communities, and ultimately, changes the world.

Are You Coachable?

Coachable people seek out those who speak truth to them, even if it is a painful truth, because it protects them and it makes them a better person and leader.

Gary Rohrmayer, pastor, author, and speaker

Effective leaders remain coachable. Many people in positions of authority or those with a title are not humble enough to be coached. Yet, humility, willingness to learn, openness to new ways or ideas—these are the first steps in being coachable.

Coachable leaders *always* practice the following:

- Invite input and feedback.
- Openly admit failures and mistakes.
- Deal with failures as learning opportunities.
- Have a written plan for growth and for increasing knowledge and leadership skills.
- Try to learn from others.

When we are coachable, we challenge ourselves to be better versions of ourselves. We are committed to our own development.

*T*ODAY, I WILL FOCUS MY ATTENTION ON THE FOLLOWING AREA OF DEVELOPMENT:

_____

_____

_____

_____

_____

_____

_____

_____

_____

_____

_____

_____

_____

I WILL DO THIS BECAUSE:

_____

_____

_____

_____

_____

Build Your Coaching Mindset

Watch your thoughts; they become your words. Watch your words; they become your actions. Watch your actions; they become your habits. Watch your habits; they become your character. Watch your character; it becomes your destiny.

Frank Outlaw, founder, BI-LO

What does your *mindset* tell you? Your mindset reflects your *past*, describes your *present*, and predicts your *future*.

Self-awareness is critical in building a positive mindset for influencing others. The four levels of self-awareness are:

- ° Knowing your thoughts.
- ° Knowing your purpose.
- ° Knowing your values.
- ° Knowing your emotions.

Developing a keen awareness at these four levels enables you to be more personally effective, authentic, and credible.

Beyond self-awareness, certain attributes go into making up an effective coach. These include being:

- ° **POSITIVE.** Start with what's working and what's good, and put energy there. People grow the most where they know the most.
- ° **ENTHUSIASTIC.** Your attitude is catchy. Project enthusiasm—and that is what you will get.
- ° **FOCUSED.** Be specific and keep the discussion on the issue.
- ° **OBSERVANT.** Open eyes and ears help in coaching.
- ° **PATIENT.** This is a coach's survival skill. We cannot change people. They change themselves; we go at their pace.
- ° **CURIOUS.** Genuine curiosity serves to make questions more authentic and opens the door to more possibilities.

TODAY, I WILL ASSESS MY COACHING MINDSET. WHERE DO I NEED TO BECOME MORE SELF-AWARE? AND IN WHICH AREAS AM I STRONGEST AND SHOULD I EMPHASIZE MOST?

_____

_____

_____

_____

_____

_____

_____

_____

_____

_____

_____

_____

_____

_____

_____

_____

I WILL DO THIS BECAUSE:

_____

_____

_____

_____

Evaluated Experience

Experience teaches nothing, but evaluated experience teaches everything.

John C. Maxwell, leadership expert and best-selling author

Experience—whether direct or what we glean from others' experiences—is our best teacher, even or maybe especially when the lessons come with hefty price tags. Yet, many people have years of experience but not much wisdom or skill to show for it. Some people learn to grow as a result of their experience; others don't. The level of assessment or evaluation after the experiences makes all the difference.

Consider this: Every day, we fill our calendars with events—appointments, meetings, classes, Zoom calls, etc. Every one of these offers us an opportunity to learn and grow, but only if we reflect on what happened. In these events, we have conversations, make plans, and make decisions—all of these should be evaluated to become learning moments, growing moments, and teaching moments that we can pass along.

As a leader, do you make the time to evaluate your experiences? Recent ones? Older ones? Will you make the time to do this?

TODAY, I WILL CONSIDER HOW WELL I HAVE BEEN REFLECTING ON AND EVALUATING MY EXPERIENCES. WHAT CAN I DO TO NUDGE MYSELF IN THE DIRECTION OF LEARNING AND GROWING FROM MY EXPERIENCE—AND HELPING OTHERS TO DO SO AS WELL?

_____

_____

_____

_____

_____

_____

_____

_____

_____

_____

_____

I WILL ASSESS HOW WELL I AM DOING AND HOW I CAN GET BETTER BECAUSE:

_____

_____

_____

_____

_____

_____

Discovery

It's what you learn after you know it all that counts.

John Wooden, legendary basketball coach

True or false: The more successful we are as leaders, the more likely we are to think we're supposed to have all the answers.

Early in my career, this was true for me—and a huge blind spot. Because I was the head person, I thought I had to have all the answers. But, of course, that was not true. Sure, in some cases, I did know things that others didn't. But even in those cases, what was more important in helping others grow was being able to guide them to discover the truth, including new concepts.

The most effective way to guide them toward discovery was to ask questions. As they were able to answer the questions, they discovered solutions for themselves. This was far more empowering for them than if I'd offered up some idea or solution.

Do this often enough and you will see a pattern emerge: Discovery leads to growth. Growth leads to improved behavior. Improved behavior leads to improved performance. Improved performance creates organization change, so that when the person grows, when people grow, the organization grows in turn.

Reflect on the times you've been given solutions versus discovered them for yourself. Which has influenced you more? What can you do to guide your people toward self-discovery and growth?

*T*ODAY, I WILL COMMIT TO CONSIDERING HOW I HAVE BENEFITED FROM DISCOVERING THINGS ON MY OWN AND HOW I MIGHT GUIDE MY TEAM TOWARD SELF-DISCOVERY AND GROWTH.

_____

_____

_____

_____

_____

_____

_____

_____

_____

_____

I WILL DO THIS BECAUSE:

_____

_____

_____

_____

_____

Your Most Important Asset

People are definitely a company's greatest asset. It doesn't make any difference whether the product is cars or cosmetics. A company is only as good as the people it keeps.

Mary Kay Ash, founder, Mary Kay Cosmetics, Inc.

I hope we have no argument with this statement: The most important asset we have is our people, though, of course, people are worth much more than all assets combined.

Leaders may be business builders, but we must first be *people* builders—people will grow the business.

There is no doubt that people development and effective coaching takes time. Our busy schedules and pressing matters can contribute to dismissing people development. Our leadership team and top performers are the most important assets we have. Therefore, investing time with them is the best investment.

Here is what I have found: Coaching and mentoring another person is about changing their thinking. When you change thinking, you change beliefs. When you change beliefs, you change expectations. When you change expectations, you change attitudes. When you change attitudes, you can change behavior. When behavior is changed, you change performance, and when you change performance, you can change a life! Who knew leaders could be life changers?!

TODAY, I WILL ASSESS HOW MUCH TIME I AM INVESTING IN MY KEY PEOPLE TO HELP THEM GROW AND CHANGE. HOW DO I NEED TO ADJUST IF I AM NOT INVESTING ENOUGH TIME—AND HOW CAN WE MAKE THE MOST OF THE TIME I AM INVESTING IN THEM?

_____

_____

_____

_____

_____

_____

_____

_____

_____

_____

I WILL EXAMINE THIS BECAUSE:

_____

_____

_____

_____

The Power
of Mentorship

There is no such thing as a "self-made" man. We are made up of thousands of others.

George Matthew Adams, newspaper columnist and syndicator

Let me ask you a question: "Did you get here alone? Are you really self-made?" Probably not. Whatever we have accomplished, it's likely the result of someone helping guide us. It may have been a coach, a boss, a co-worker, a teacher or a parent—or maybe several people depending on your stage of life.

As leaders, we make investments and decisions on a daily basis. When we decide to invest our time in mentoring someone, we expand the enterprise—we help evolve it.

In the book *The Leadership Challenge,* authors James M. Kouzes and Barry Z. Posner write, "Leaders are pioneers; they guide us to new and often unfamiliar destinations. Leaders move us forward."

The positive result of mentoring is people growth. And we know that people growth equals business growth.

Are you mentoring someone? Someone is waiting.

$\mathcal{T}$ODAY, I WILL CONSIDER HOW I HAVE BEEN MENTORED. WHAT WENT WELL? WHAT COULD HAVE GONE BETTER? AND HOW CAN I USE THIS KNOWLEDGE TO BECOME A BETTER MENTOR?

_____

_____

_____

_____

_____

_____

_____

_____

_____

_____

_____

_____

_____

_____

_____

I WILL DO THIS BECAUSE:

_____

_____

_____

_____

In teaching, it is the method and not the content that is the message, the drawing it out, not pumping it in.

Ashley Montagu, anthropologist and writer

One-to-one coaching is an opportunity to change behavior and yield positive results. I have found that my preparation for coaching sessions is critical. Remember—our intention is always to help our team members increase productivity.

I suggest taking a few minutes prior to each session to prepare by doing the following:

- Review previous coaching sessions. Get a feel for where the person is, including strengths and areas in need of improvement.
- Write down open-ended questions. Use active inquiry and active listening. When executed properly, your team will experience discovery learning.
- Visualize your team performing on the level you want them to.

Three factors influence people's productivity:

- The degree to which you sincerely believe they can achieve higher performance.
- The degree to which they believe that you believe in them.
- The degree to which there is trust, mutual respect and rapport between you and them.

TODAY, I WILL CONSIDER HOW WELL I PREPARE FOR COACHING SESSIONS WITH MY TEAM. AND I WILL CHECK MYSELF—HOW WELL I AM DRAWING THEM OUT, HOW WELL I TRULY BELIEVE IN THEIR CAPACITY TO IMPROVE, AS WELL AS OUR SHARED TRUST, RESPECT, AND RAPPORT. ANYWHERE I AM FALLING SHORT, I WILL DETERMINE HOW I CAN CHANGE.

_____

_____

_____

_____

_____

_____

_____

_____

_____

_____

I WILL DO THIS BECAUSE:

_____

_____

_____

_____

People soon discover the level of performance that their managers will settle for and gravitate to that level. Managers then assume that's all that people are capable of achieving, so they accept it as fact and quit challenging their people to get better. So, each reinforces what the other believes.

Ron Willingham on the "Law of Limited Performance" in *The People Principle*

A stereotype of coaches of athletes is that of the hard-driving go-getter who wants to extract all from his or her team. But, when we are in coaching mode, we may often be too rough. We think we need to impart every last drop of *our* wisdom, and this places us in the position of "instructor" rather than a partner in their learning.

Instead, we can adopt the following practices and modes:

- Prior to our coaching session, identify the purpose.
- Plan to measure them against themselves and not others.
- Accept your thinking partners as they are and practice discovery learning by asking questions that are clear, brief, focused, relevant, constructive and, of course, open ended. You can even plan some questions in advance, so long as you are prepared to shift to meet the needs of your thinking partner.
- Through discovery learning, challenge them to short-term goals, with commitments from them on specific activities and behavior changes; a short time frame and target can help bolster their confidence with a victory, and victories create momentum toward improvement.

$\mathcal{T}$ODAY, I WILL FOCUS ON MY SPECIFIC COACHING PRACTICES: WHAT AM
I DOING WELL, AND WHERE COULD I USE SELF-DISCOVERY AND SHORT-TERM
GOALS TO MAKE CHANGES?

_____

_____

_____

_____

_____

_____

_____

_____

_____

_____

_____

_____

I WILL DO THIS BECAUSE:

_____

_____

_____

_____

In my years of coaching, I have observed that extraordinary leaders all have one trait in common: deep convictions about helping others to improve. This is their heartbeat. They have mastered the skills and disciplines needed to help others reach peak levels of performance. This is one of their primary areas of focus.

Daniel Harkavy in *Becoming a Coaching Leader*

Identifying performance and personal-life gaps. Affirming gifts. Uncovering convictions and encouraging vision consistent with the convictions. Helping create plans for success. Maintaining focus and helping align actions with plans. Pinpointing and assessing resources. Offering a fresh perspective toward actions and goal completions. Keeping the team to account. These are all the things a coaching leader does.

Yet, too often, our thinking partners may be overly anxious and cannot see potential solutions or opportunities that beat a path toward their goals.

When we coach, we can break things down along these steps:

ASK about their goals and objectives. What specific ones are they working on and where are they? What's keeping them from reaching the goal or goals? What skills or behaviors will help them move through these constraints?

LISTEN without distractions or interruptions (make sure your phone is off). What are their words, tone, body language? Question them to help them uncover the answers. And believe that they have the answers; they are just waiting to be discovered.

COACH by confronting the constraints and problem areas without criticism or negativity. Suggest one action that will help them remove a constraint and move them toward a goal. Keep the responsibility on them.

PRAISE by pointing out specific talents, skills, attitudes, knowledge, or abilities that will help them reach their goals. Express your belief they will do whatever it takes to succeed. Explain potential you see in them that they may not see in themselves.

CHALLENGE them to become their best. Ask them to commit to specific goals, results, and time frames. Explain that you will follow up and keep them accountable. Thank them and remind them how important they are to your team.

Today, I will examine the overall tenor of my coaching sessions. How am I practicing asking, listening, coaching, praising, and challenging? Am I following through on my commitments to my learning partners?

_____

_____

_____

_____

_____

_____

_____

_____

_____

_____

_____

_____

_____

I WILL DO THIS BECAUSE:

_____

_____

_____

_____

The Essentials
of Mentorship

MASTERPIECE [79]

*The ultimate leader is one who is willing to develop people to the point
they surpass him or her in knowledge or ability.*

Fred Manske, Jr., author, *Secrets of Effective Leadership*

To me, a mentor and a coach share many of the same qualities, yet a mentor can be someone I have never met. For example, I count late UCLA basketball coach John Wooden as one of my mentors. A mentor can be someone you work with periodically, but perhaps that person is not actively coaching. Whereas a coach helps the person being coached discover what they need to grow and does this on a regular basis.

Several characteristics make effective mentors and coaches:

WISDOM. There is no substitute for experience. Your past successes and failures are your bank account for being an effective mentor.

EMPATHY. Chances are you were mentored and can relate to the place the mentee is in.

PATIENCE. Growing and developing people takes time. If you are not willing to invest the time needed, you simply cannot be effective at mentoring.

SKILL. As the mentor, you are equipped and likely above average at the critical skills required to do the job. Your measurable success will give you credibility.

Your mentee will ask themselves if you have the experience, but your empathy and patience will drive the relationship.

TODAY, I WILL COMMIT TO ASSESSING MY WISDOM, EMPATHY, PATIENCE, AND SKILL IN MENTORING OTHERS. WHICH AREA OR AREAS DO I NEED TO WORK ON TO BECOME A BETTER MENTOR, AND HOW WILL I DO THIS?

_____

_____

_____

_____

_____

_____

_____

_____

_____

_____

_____

_____

_____

_____

I WILL DO THIS BECAUSE:

_____

_____

_____

_____

How Equipped Is Your Team?

A great person attracts great people and knows how to hold them together.
Johann Wolfgang von Goethe, poet, playwright, and natural scientist

All leaders desire to have high-performing, winning teams, and it all starts with selecting the right people and putting them in the right seats. The next step is to be certain they are properly equipped to get the desired results.

My friend and mentor John Maxwell says, "We must CARE for our people in order to equip them."

> Communication
> Affirmation
> Recognition
> Example

Additionally, I have found we must provide certain resources in order to equip them best. Ask yourself the following questions:

- Is my environment conducive for growth?
- Do I have an education and training environment?
- Do I have an accountability process?

Once you have identified your team's strengths, emphasize those and fight to keep them in their strength zone. Manage their weaknesses and provide them with the tools needed to succeed. Remember—everyone wants to feel valued. Everyone wants to be encouraged, so be their CEO, their Chief Encouragement Officer.

TODAY, I WILL ASSESS HOW WELL I AM EQUIPPING MY TEAM. AM I USING
CARE WITH THEM? AND, HOW IS OUR ENVIRONMENT AND TRAINING?
IS OUR ACCOUNTABILITY PROCESS THE BEST IT CAN BE SO THAT THEY KNOW
WHERE THEY STAND?

_____

_____

_____

_____

_____

_____

_____

_____

_____

_____

_____

_____

I WILL EXAMINE THIS BECAUSE:

_____

_____

_____

_____

Encouragement
Is Key

Flatter me, and I may not believe you, criticize me, and I may not like you, ignore me, and I may not forgive you. Encourage me, and I will not forget you.

William Arthur Ward, motivational writer

Every person on the planet wants to believe they have value. They want to know that they matter and that they count for something. It is my belief that being valued and mattered is a basic human need.

As a leader, helping someone feel significant can be a game changer.

If you ever played sports, you know how important the words of encouragement coming from the coach were to you. Maybe accompanied with a pat on the back, or fist pump, the words and the actions made you feel valued, needed, and worth the investment of their time and energy.

I'll bet you have people in your organization right now who are looking for encouragement. They want to know that what they're doing matters and how it's positively impacting the organization. Find those people, and thank them. Encourage them. Help them grow, for they will help your organization prosper.

$\mathcal{T}$ODAY, I WILL CONSIDER WHERE I AM IN TERMS OF PROVIDING
CONSISTENT ENCOURAGEMENT TO MY TEAM. WHO IS THE ONE PERSON
I CAN ENCOURAGE TODAY?

_____

AND HOW WILL I DO THAT?

_____
_____
_____
_____
_____
_____
_____
_____
_____
_____
_____

I WILL DO THIS BECAUSE:

_____
_____
_____
_____

Be a Leader.
Be a Giver.

You give but little when you give of your possessions. It is when you give of yourself that you truly give.

Khalil Gibran, poet and philosopher

As leaders, we have the privilege to give in many ways. Our generosity is not limited to our financial resources. There is no better feeling than to give your resources to another person and to causes in need—and the generosity tends to reproduce itself. When one candle lights another, the light doubles.

We can give our time and energy to causes. Volunteerism is our honor and privilege. Organizations, whether they be civic, charitable, or industry, need effective leaders. We all have the time. The old saying is true: "Busy people get things done." Our communities need our wisdom, talents, and skills to guide and direct the impact of our organization.

We should always be mentoring. We should always be helping another person grow, succeed, and find their true passion. Remember: "All that is not given is lost."

I'm learning that true generosity is a *heart* thing. Giving for the right reason—unconditionally, with no expected return—must come from the heart. Giving and generosity are perpetually in season. So, find organizations you can help, people you can mentor, and give of your time, talents and support. Leadership always extends beyond the boardroom and into our communities.

_T_ODAY, I WILL CONTEMPLATE HOW I AM SHARING MY TIME, TALENTS, AND SUPPORT —WITH MY TEAM AND BEYOND OUR ORGANIZATION. WHO NEEDS MORE?

_____

_____

AND WHERE CAN I STEP IT UP?

_____

_____

_____

_____

_____

_____

_____

_____

_____

I WILL DO THIS BECAUSE:

_____

_____

_____

_____

How to Maximize Your
Strengths-Based Team

The task of leadership is not to put greatness into people, but to elicit it, for the greatness is there already.

John Buchan, politician and author

Most of us are familiar with the Jim Collins quote, "Get the right people on the bus in the right seats." A winning coach on a sports team would never put a player in a position where they do not leverage his or her strengths, yet we often experience this in the workplace. So, how can we fix this?

To maximize the productivity of individual team members, consider the following:

- Identify what success looks like. What are the outcomes you want? Is each function/role among the team members clearly defined?
- Once success is defined, develop a list of expected skill sets and behaviors needed to get results.
- Assess your team members' strengths. Several tools exist to help you in determining strengths. I like the assessment tool Strengths Finder 2.0, created by Tom Rath and the Gallup organization (rebranded as CliftonStrengths).
- Align the right people with the right job. Now it's time to play the matching game: Compare the required skill sets of each role with the strengths of the individuals on the team. The question to ask: "Are my people in roles in which they can leverage their strengths?"

As leaders, it is our responsibility to ensure we have the right people for the right jobs, not just the company. Fitting in culturally is a great attribute, but employees also have to demonstrate aptitude, success in their roles. If they aren't, it's our job to fix the problem, which can sometimes mean finding new talent.

*T*ODAY, I WILL ASSESS WHETHER I HAVE THE RIGHT PEOPLE IN THE RIGHT ROLES TO ENSURE THAT THE GREATNESS THAT IS PRESENT IS MADE MANIFEST. ARE THE ROLES AND ACCOMPANYING SKILL SETS AND BEHAVIORS CLEARLY DEFINED?

_____

_____

_____

_____

_____

HOW WELL DO I UNDERSTAND THE STRENGTHS OF EACH MEMBER OF MY TEAM TO ENSURE WE ARE WORKING TO OUR BEST ADVANTAGE?

_____

_____

_____

_____

_____

I WILL DO THIS BECAUSE:

_____

_____

_____

_____

Create a Culture
of Accountability

With a company full of accountable people, extraordinary things, even the entirely unexpected, tend to happen.

Roger Connors, management consultant and author

What does a high-accountability culture—the kind found in high-performance teams— look like? A common denominator is that in accountability cultures, everyone holds each other accountable for their commitments in a positive and productive manner. Team members will not let their teammates down, and therefore, they perform well and create a culture of high productivity and typically successful outcomes.

This does not happen overnight; the culture evolves from one person or event to the next. One thing that can slow down this process is accountability gaps. Be aware of these. In many cases, we are responsible for the gap. I have committed this sin. When assigning a task or a project, I have been at fault for not being clear on expectations or not being clear on what success looks like when it is completed.

Identifying and communicating metrics are key to overall project/task success, and it's our job to share those with our team. I've been guilty of not setting clear deadlines as well as being vague in my delivery with phrases like, "Get this report to me as soon as you can." That has come back to sting me.

We need to be aware of ambiguities when we assign tasks, projects, or other work with deadlines. In addition, we can't allow employees to skate away with vagueness. The result could be failure.

Here are some of the biggest offenders from the Glossary of Failure:

- Soon
- ASAP
- Right away
- I'll get on it
- Later
- Try
- Should
- Might

There are three important rules in creating an accountability culture: specificity, specificity, specificity. Here are some examples:

- What date and time can I follow up with you to close the loop?
- Who owns it?
- This is what success looks like...

Scrub "should" and "might" from your vocabulary and replace them with "will."

- What could get in your way?

TODAY, I WILL CHECK MYSELF ON HOW I AM MINDING MY TEAM'S ACCOUNTABILITY GAPS. AM I USING VAGUE LANGUAGE WHEN MAKING ASSIGNMENTS? ARE TEAM MEMBERS THEMSELVES BEING VAGUE IN COMMITTING TO DEADLINES—AND AM I LETTING THEM GET AWAY WITH THAT?

_____

_____

_____

_____

_____

_____

HOW WELL AM I PRESENTING WHAT SUCCESS LOOKS AND FEELS LIKE?

_____

_____

_____

_____

_____

_____

I WILL DO THIS BECAUSE:

_____

_____

_____

_____

Inspire Your
Team to Persevere

Indomitable perseverance in a business, properly understood, always ensures ultimate success.

Cyrus McCormick, inventor and industrialist

I have been reflecting on the story of Sir Ernest Shackleton. He led the entire crew of his ship, *Endurance,* to safety after being marooned on an ice floe for 15 months. Forced to abandon his original plan to cross the Antarctic, Shackleton's story holds strong lessons for leaders facing uncontrollable change.

Here are a few of his actions that you can put in place today that helped his people—and will help yours—keep the faith during periods of upheaval:

REDEFINE ACHIEVABLE GOALS.

People need clear goals to keep their spirits and productivity up. Shackleton told his crew they would live on the ice pack until it broke up and then use the ship's lifeboats to sail to safety.

ASSIGN ROUTINE TASKS.

Fifteen months on an ice floe would drive anyone crazy. Shackleton assigned daily tasks that supported the long-term goal of eventual freedom.

DEMONSTRATE UNITY.

Shackleton, the ship's captain, and other expedition leaders lived and worked alongside everyone. They were a team and exemplified the mantra of, "We're in this together."

TODAY, I WILL ASSESS HOW WELL I AM INSPIRING MY TEAM TO KEEP AT IT.
HOW WELL DO I USE TIMES OF GREAT CHANGE TO REDEFINE GOALS WE
CAN ACHIEVE, TO GIVE EVERYONE ROUTINE TASKS, AND TO GET INTO THE
TRENCHES WITH THEM, TO THE EXTENT I CAN?

_____

_____

_____

_____

_____

_____

WHAT MORE CAN I DO TO HELP US PERSEVERE?

_____

_____

_____

_____

_____

I WILL DO THIS BECAUSE:

_____

_____

_____

_____

Mining for Gold

Trust people and they will be true to you; treat them greatly and they will show themselves great.

Ralph Waldo Emerson, essayist, poet, philosopher, and abolitionist

Scottish-born Andrew Carnegie came to America as a boy. He did a variety of small jobs. Eventually, he ended up at the largest steel manufacturer in the United States, becoming for a time the wealthiest man in America as well as a great philanthropist.

At one point during his career, he had 43 millionaires working for him. In the late 1800s, a millionaire was rare. A reporter once asked Carnegie how he managed to hire 43 millionaires. Carnegie replied, "They were not millionaires when I hired them."

The reporter's follow-up question was simple, yet provocative: "How did you develop them to be so valuable that they would accumulate that much wealth?"

Carnegie's response: "People are developed the same way that gold is mined. When gold is mined, several tons of dirt must be removed to get an ounce of gold, but one doesn't go in the mine looking for dirt—one goes in looking for gold."

Leaders who see their purpose as looking for the gold in their people end up with the richest outcome: a team of talented, committed individuals who inspire all of us to look for the gold.

TODAY, I WILL EVALUATE HOW INTENTLY I AM SEEKING—AND WHETHER
I AM FINDING—THE GOLD IN MY TEAM MEMBERS. IF I HAVE BEEN ABLE TO DO
THIS, WHAT KINDS OF RESULTS ARE WE SEEING?

_____
_____
_____
_____
_____
_____
_____
_____
_____

IF NOT, HOW DO I NEED TO CHANGE TO HELP US ALL FIND THE GOLD?

_____
_____
_____
_____

I WILL EVALUATE THIS BECAUSE:

_____
_____
_____
_____

What Are
You Tracking?

Good managers don't set a goal to increase efficiency, but rather an implementation of business process improvements that result in higher efficiency as well.

Eraldo Banovac, energy expert advisor and author

As leaders, we know how important it is to track results. Without results, we have no business. To keep the ball rolling, we need the action that drives results.

To be clear, I'm not referring to our people being busy or looking busy, but rather doing the right actions that drive results. Take sales as an example. We measure sales, and we obviously need new business, a growing market share, etc., but these do not necessarily drive results; these only measure results.

What we must have is accountability that drives results. Put another way, when coaching your team and when reviewing the list of the activities they can control, help them identify the ones that actually affect the outcomes you want. Without emphasizing this, it's easy to get pulled into the "I'm too busy" trap.

So, do not count the score; count the behaviors that run up the score, because what gets the attention and focus are the things that get done.

$\mathcal{T}$ODAY, I WILL TAKE AN HONEST LOOK AT WHAT WE ARE TRACKING.
IS OUR FOCUS ON RESULTS ALONE—OR THE BEHAVIORS AND ACTIVITIES
THAT PUSH THE RESULTS?

_____

_____

_____

_____

_____

WHEN I AM COACHING, AM I CAREFULLY LOOKING AT THE ACTIONS WITHIN
MY TEAM'S CONTROL, THE ONES THAT ELICIT GREAT RESULTS?

_____

_____

_____

_____

_____

IF NOT, HOW DO I NEED TO SHIFT THIS?

_____

_____

_____

I WILL EVALUATE THIS BECAUSE:

_____

_____

Control = Results

There is only one way to happiness and that is to cease worrying about things which are beyond the power of our will.

Epictetus, Stoic philosopher

Football fans may have heard of Tony Dungy. He became the head coach of the Tampa Bay Buccaneers in 1996. The team had 13 losing seasons behind them, and friends tried to persuade Dungy not to take the job. He did anyway.

When he arrived, all he heard was excuses: poor stadium, low ticket sales, couldn't win away games if the weather was cold, not drafting the right players. Here is the best one: Apparently, a voodoo-practicing woman, who had loved quarterback Doug Williams, put a curse on the team when he left.

When Dungy examined the list of obstacles for not winning, he realized something important —the entire list was outside the players' control. He immediately did something that all great leaders do. He asked a powerful question, "What factors do we control that will contribute to our success?"

He then researched what winning teams were doing more than most. He discovered what he knew all along: they focused on what they could control.

We can best help our team, our mentees, by helping them understand what they can control. Gaining this understanding affects results and empowers them to exercise that control, which will also keep them focused on the right activities.

TODAY, I WILL CONSIDER WHETHER I MYSELF MAINTAIN FOCUS ON THINGS WITHIN MY CONTROL OR WHETHER MY ATTENTION RUNS TO THINGS BEYOND MY CONTROL. I WILL ASSESS HOW THIS IMPEDES MY WORK, AND I WILL ALSO LOOK AT HOW I CAN SHIFT AND HOW I CAN SUPPORT MY TEAM MEMBERS IN REFOCUSING THEIR ATTENTION ON THE ACTIVITIES THEY CAN CONTROL.

_____

_____

_____

_____

_____

_____

_____

_____

_____

_____

_____

_____

I WILL DO THIS BECAUSE:

_____

_____

_____

_____

Do Your Key People
Feel Known and Valued?

The role of a creative leader is not to have all the ideas; it's to create a culture where everyone can have ideas and feel that they're valued.

Sir Ken Robinson, creativity consultant, educator, author, and speaker

If someone were to ask you if your key people knew you valued them, how would you answer? A business owner I asked recently said, "Of course they feel valued."

But in our deeper dive, he shamefully admitted he wasn't connecting with his best. He said, "I think I was subconsciously taking them for granted." He admitted he was doing more talking and not as much listening.

My experience in working with my best is something I pulled from the experience of an older friend, who owned a business that made machinery for imprinting items, from dashboards to golf bags. He spent three days visiting their Mexican distribution center to call on customers with the salesperson. My friend had ranked the customers by the amount of business provided. The salesperson wanted to start with those who accounted for the least. Finally, my friend intervened and they shifted their visits to top-tier customers. The lesson: Focus on those who increase your success.

In my own work, I had not been paying attention to my top producers. After I shifted, I never had anyone say, "Bob, leave me alone." Rather, if I had not talked with one of them in a couple of weeks, they would point this out.

Now when I work with leaders, I have them place customers into tiers and make sure they're loving on their Tier 1 people. I ask them to consider what it would take to move their top Tier 2 customers to Tier 1.

This works because, embedded deep in our DNA, humans want to feel connected, known, and valued—not taken for granted. Feeling connected is critical for the human soul. Care needs to be taken when creating an atmosphere of connection while maintaining professional relationships. The answer in most cases is: ask more questions.

Here are some questions to consider in your one-to-one coaching: What is one frustration you are experiencing? Where are you experiencing the most stress? What can I do to help you accomplish your goals? What do I need to do to communicate more clearly? How are you feeling about work/life balance? What do you feel we should stop doing that is no longer working?

Bottom line, they will feel known and valued, which could improve the bottom line.

TODAY, I WILL TAKE A HARD LOOK AT HOW I AM VALUING MY TEAM.
AM I NOT ASKING ENOUGH OR NOT ASKING OPEN-ENDED DISCOVERY QUESTIONS?
TALKING MORE THAN LISTENING?

_____

_____

_____

_____

_____

_____

_____

IF SO, WHAT DO I NEED TO DO TO SHIFT?

_____

_____

_____

IF I AM MAKING MY TEAM FEEL VALUED, WHAT MORE CAN I DO?

_____

_____

_____

I WILL EXAMINE THIS BECAUSE:

_____

_____

_____

The Stagecoach
Leader

Managers help people see themselves as they are; leaders help people to see themselves better than they are.

Jim Rohn, author, speaker, and personal-development pioneer

Some folks reading this may not remember or be able to identify a stagecoach. When I was a youngster during the early days of TV, Westerns were popular. Every Western seemed to have a stagecoach. And stagecoaches moved people.

As leaders, we also move people, because we help develop people. Of course, you could have a stagecoach with a loose wheel or one with a horse whose tack is ill-fitting, which means we can always be open to improvement. Good coaching leaders, among other things:

- Are always moving, growing, and improving (serving as an example).
- See people for what they can become, not as they are.
- Never accept the status quo.
- Help their teams identify gaps and lead them to solutions.
- Recognize and affirm the talents and skills of teammates.
- Hold teammates accountable to their commitments.
- Help teammates see their role in the big picture.
- Are not afraid to empower an individual or the team.

In a meeting with a C Suite executive, we discussed the lack of performance of one of his key players. (A reminder: Money is not always the chief motivator.) I asked him if he knew what motivates this person. He looked back at me with an almost apologetic embarrassed look and said, "In all honesty, Bob, I don't."

Leaders can't move people if they don't know them. Connecting at the heart level is key to moving people. Beyond that, good coaching leaders help others win by helping them to discover the knowledge, strategies, and action plans for better results. When our team moves from good to great, just imagine how our businesses flow and grow!

TODAY, I WILL TAKE A LOOK AT HOW WELL I AM MOVING MY TEAM.
DO I KNOW WHAT MOTIVATES THEM, AND AM I HELPING THEM TO ACHIEVE
WHAT THEY WANT?

_____

_____

_____

_____

_____

HOW WELL AM I HELPING THEM IDENTIFY GAPS AND DISCOVER SOLUTIONS?
WHAT AM I DOING TO EMPOWER THEM?

_____

_____

_____

_____

I WILL EXAMINE THIS BECAUSE:

_____

_____

_____

_____

The Power
of Influence

Power is a tool, influence is a skill; one is a fist, the other a fingertip.

Nancy Gibbs, journalist

Influence effectiveness is partly a function of the influencer's—the leader's—skill in a number of areas, such as communication and reasoning. To further break this down, we can consider the following:

LOGICAL REASONING. The ability to think logically, analyze problems, and identify logical solutions.

PROBING. Asking insightful questions that lead others to the heart of the problem or issue.

LISTENING. Actively listening to others; being all in—engaged with others when they are speaking and accurately hearing and retaining their comments.

FINDING CREATIVE ALTERNATIVES. Being able to see creative solutions where others haven't (thinking outside the box).

Influence effectiveness is also a function of interpersonal skills. These include:

BEING GENUINE. Being authentic in showing care and concern for and curiosity about other people. Making others feel important and understood. (Is this not what we all want?)

INSIGHT INTO WHAT OTHERS VALUE. Having a strong intuitive understanding of others and what is important to them.

SENSITIVITY FOR THE FEELINGS OF OTHERS. Understanding human emotions and empathizing with people without developing emotional attachment.

RAPPORT AND TRUST. Establishing trusting connections, building harmony in relationships, and conveying confidence that you, too, can be trusted.

Of course, it takes practice and time to perfect these skills, but every day provides us an opportunity to practice influence.

TODAY, I WILL ASSESS MY INFLUENCE EFFECTIVENESS BY TAKING A LOOK AT HOW WELL I AM AT COMMUNICATING, REASONING, AND DEMONSTRATING MY CARE AND EMPATHY FOR MY TEAM. I WILL DO THIS BY:

_____

_____

_____

_____

_____

_____

_____

_____

_____

_____

_____

_____

_____

I WILL DO THIS BECAUSE:

_____

_____

_____

_____

_____

_____

Influence Is about Them —the Responsibility Is Ours

Blessed influence of one true loving human soul on another! Not calculable by algebra, not deducible by logic, but mysterious, effectual, mighty as the hidden process by which the tiny seed is quickened, and bursts forth into tall stem and broad leaf, and glowing tasseled flower.

George Eliot, novelist, poet, journalist, and translator

My mentor, John Maxwell, teaches that the definition of leadership is influence, and your influence of another person is critical in your leadership. Yet, influence is *not* about you. Influence is the experience you create for someone based on what they see, hear, and understand. This means the responsibility shifts from the listener or reader to the communicator. That is, we must earn the right for people to listen to us.

We influence people by *what we say* and *how we make them feel*. It is important we connect with them, engage with them in a way they feel that it is about them, not about our agenda. And while those we influence do benefit, we have got to own and continue to develop the skills required to influence and change behavior to get better results.

There are certain qualities and characteristics we need to possess and to develop in order to maintain influence. We need to be:

- Trustworthy
- Credible
- Confident
- Passionate
- Authentic
- Consistent
- Caring
- Knowledgeable

We grow and evolve these traits through daily usage, which then flows into further influence.

*T*ODAY, I WILL TAKE A LOOK AT MY ATTITUDE TOWARD THE ROLE OF INFLUENCE IN MY LEADERSHIP AND HOW THAT INFLUENCE AFFECTS INDIVIDUAL TEAM MEMBERS AND OUR ORGANIZATION AS A WHOLE. I WILL ASSESS HOW WELL I AM DAILY EXPRESSING THE QUALITIES THAT SUPPORT INFLUENCE. WHERE CAN I IMPROVE?

_____

_____

_____

_____

_____

_____

_____

_____

HOW WILL I DO THIS?

_____

_____

_____

_____

I WILL DO THIS BECAUSE:

_____

_____

_____

_____

ACKNOWLEDGMENTS

All of our journeys start long before our conception, long before we take our first breath. For me, the journey to where I am began, in part, with my grandparents who lived in Sicily, in a small mountain town of 1,200 people south of Palermo. My high school sweetheart and wife of 56 years, Patty, and I were fortunate to have the opportunity a few years ago to travel to Sicily and visit the town. We went to the church where my grandparents were born and married. The inspiration for me to write this book came to me that day. I couldn't help but think there was a particular day that my grandfather made a decision to emigrate to the United States. More than 120 years ago, my grandfather decided to leave the village, take a train to Palermo and a boat to Ellis Island, and that is where my story—my masterpiece—then intersected with so many millions of others.

We can never predict the impact—small or large—of our decisions upon others, but each decision we make does have an impact. In the case of my grandparents, they cannot know how many thousands of lives they have touched just through this one grandson.

As with any major project in life, the people who have contributed are of the utmost importance. This book is certainly no exception. The inspiration for this book came from many people in my life. Collectively, they have helped shape my beliefs, values and philosophy on personal growth and leadership development. With that said, I would like to offer my deepest gratitude to the following people who came along on this journey with me. I could not have done it with them.

First of all, Patty. We were so young, and maybe not too bright, but it worked. Patty's dedication and faithfulness to all my crazy ideas and dreams have had such a profound impact on me. I hope she knows that, knows how much love her and how grateful I am for her accompanying me.

My parents. Neither one had a high school education, yet both taught my brother and me about working hard for what we want, and that we are not entitled to anything unless we have earned it. I have intended to live that out and pay it forward.

To my children and grandchildren. You have been a true blessing to me. Your love and devotion to our family has encouraged me to be the best example I could be. With love and gratitude.

To my Masterpiece Team. Leigh Glenn, Brittany Frey, and Bill Zulewski for your commitment and dedication to see this project through, despite all of the rabbit trails I took you down. I am forever grateful.

So many people have inspired me to grow and become a better leader. Some of them were intentional and others didn't know I existed—however, I knew them through their books, videos, workshops, tapes (yes, cassettes, video—remember, I'm "old school"). These include authors and luminaries such as the following:

John Wooden who said, "It is what you learn after you know it all that counts."

Mahatma Gandhi: "Live like you are going to die tomorrow. Learn like you are going to live forever." These quotations inspired me to become a life-long learner.

And then there are mentors, who, through their writing, have passed along wonderful insights into The Art of Leadership. I thank them for the words they have shared: Stephen Covey, Zig Ziglar, Brian Tracy, Peter Drucker, Jim Collins, Dale Carnegie, Simon Sinek, Patrick Lencioni, Dr. Henry Cloud, Ken Blanchard, Robin Sharma. There are many more.

The following people I have known and consider them mentors. They have since passed and will never be forgotten. They have made a lasting imprint.

Fran Morgan: He taught me how to mentor someone, on his porch, in the evenings. Fran never knew how those evenings would make such an impact on me. Fran, you were special.

Bill Moxley: He taught me to "Inspect what I expect" and maintain a standard of excellence. Bill, your backing me financially to start our company has truly impacted many lives and has been a great vote of confidence. Thanks, Bill.

Leo Futia: A humble man of character who said many times, "There is no right way to do a wrong thing." I have intended to live that out Leo—thanks.

Ron Willingham: He modeled and mentored grace, humility and a people mindset. Thanks, Ron, for modeling a person of character.

The following mentors are alive and in my life today:

John Maxwell: To this very day, you inspire me to be an influence and add value to others. I am grateful for your friendship, John.

Pastor Tom (Coach) Mullins: You inspire me to think big, that there is always a better way. Your example of how to transition Christ Fellowship Church to Todd has made a difference. I love you, Coach, and am grateful you are in my life.

I have had the privilege to be a part of a wonderful organization, GAMA International, now known by a newer name, Finseca. Two excellent Leaders who I met and became friends with through GAMA are Bob Savage and Phil Richards. You gentlemen in your own style and way have had a profound impact on elevating my leadership in building an organization. You both made a difference in my life. I am forever grateful.

And to the people of Alliance Advisory Group, I am forever grateful as well. You have honored me with the opportunity to lead and partner with you for 42-plus years. Every day, you challenged me to be the best version of me. Thank you for the opportunity.